Patons
A Story of Handknitting

Patons
A Story of Handknitting

Michael Harvey

SPRINGWOOD BOOKS
ASCOT

Copyright © Patons & Baldwins Limited 1985
All rights reserved

First published 1985
by Springwood Books Limited
Springwood House, The Avenue, Ascot, Berkshire

ISBN 0 86254 117 4

Designed by Michael R. Carter

Typeset in 11 on 12 point Italia Book
Printed in Great Britain by
Jolly & Barber Limited, Rugby
and bound by Butler & Tanner Limited, Frome

Contents

Preface		7
1	The Birth of a Craft	9
2	Knitting, Religion and the Guilds	16
3	European Traditions Develop	23
4	A Cloud on the Horizon	35
5	Co-existence and Survival	40
6	Countries Apart: Mr Baldwin in England, Mr Paton in Scotland	47
7	The Craft Becomes a Hobby	55
8	Growth on Both Sides of the Border	68
9	An Industry Geared to a Pastime	80
10	Patons Around the World	91
11	Around the Coastline	101
12	The Island Knitters	109
13	Patons and Fashion in Handknitting	118
Postscript: What Will the Future Bring?		143

ACKNOWLEDGEMENTS

Patons & Baldwins Limited and the Author wish to thank the following sources for permission to reproduce the photographs. If we have failed to trace any copyright holders, we apologise.

By courtesy and kind permission of Aero Pictorial Ltd; Airviews (M/C) Ltd, Altrincham; BBC Hulton Picture Library; The Bettman Archive; The Bude Historical & Folk Exhibition; Camera Press; Stanley D. Chapman from *The Early Factory Masters* published by David & Charles; Rae Compton from *Practical Knitting* published by Hamlyn Publishing Group; The Hudson Bay Co.; The International Wool Secretariat; Sue Leighton-White from her collection; Mr J. E. Manners; The Marquess of Salisbury; Karen McKechnie from *A Border Woollen Town* published by Longmans; Norfolk Museums Service (Strangers' Hall Museum, Norwich); The Paslod Research Fund Ltd; Trustees of the Science Museum; Scottish Fisheries Museum, Anstruther, Fife; The Shetland Museum; State of Vermont, Division for Historic Preservation, Montpelier, Vermont; Mary Thomas from her *Knitting Book* published by Hodder & Stoughton; The Board of Trustees of the Victoria and Albert Museum; Mr Heinz Zinram.

Preface

The craft of handknitting, which probably started over 2,000 years ago, is to-day very much alive and is practised throughout the world, meeting the creative and leisure needs of many. It has become a thriving business, currently contributing much to the field of fashion, and with its own particular retailing expertise.

It seemed appropriate in the year in which Patons & Baldwins Limited celebrates its two hundredth anniversary to publish a book which outlines the history of handknitting from the early days, highlights the key features in its development and explains something of the craft and industry as we now know it. The evolution and role of Patons & Baldwins Limited, in the United Kingdom and overseas, is described in a number of chapters.

We asked Michael Harvey to write this book because of his wide knowledge of handknitting including the social and economic history, design and the practice of retailing. He also has had a close relationship with our Company over many years. He has amassed an enormous amount of information and illustrations, of which only a part can be published here. We hope this book will appeal to many and that the cost will enable anyone interested in the craft, or the Company, to enjoy it, including past and present employees, handknitting retailers and young people entering the industry. Michael Harvey has been helped in his formidable task by many experts and eminent authorities as well as colleagues and friends.

The result we believe goes some way to describing how the craft of handknitting and its associated manufacturing and retail industries have reached the position of importance they hold today. Its wealth of information and copious illustrations make it a pleasure to read for the expert and the novice alike.

Knitting is fashion — it is also part of our way of life.

Alistair L. Henderson
MANAGING DIRECTOR

CHAPTER 1
The Birth of a Craft

The history of man has many fascinating pages. Those on handknitting may be little known, but they are far from being unworthy of our attention. From its beginning the craft has had its ups and downs and on more than one occasion it has seemed to be on the verge of extinction. Yet doggedly it has survived. Handknitting may have been overshadowed from time to time by seemingly more important crafts, but sound economic reasons, as well as aesthetic considerations, have ensured its continued existence.

Survival was uppermost in the thoughts of man and woman in their early days. Inevitably, food was crucial for this, but shelter and clothing came a close second. Once the basic techniques associated with survival had been mastered, security became important – and men and women began to form groups. A limited form of specialisation developed as work was divided; some would hunt or grow food, others would look after the domestic arrangements. The group would also develop family and social functions. Textiles were developed as an economic activity with an increasing social importance. In the Middle East, where it is suggested that handknitting began, tents, perhaps with knitted flaps, helped to make the cold nights more tolerable. The sandal sock made outerfoot coverings easier to bear.

Creativity evolved in the form of arts and crafts which were not merely utilitarian, but included the production of objects for their own artistic sake, such as textiles and clothing made for religious purposes or for display. Knitting paralleled these developments, as a trade developed in handknitted goods with social implications arising from communal 'knitting sittings'.

It has a fascinating history, yet it is very much alive, as witnessed by the fact that hundreds of thousands of knitters ply their needles today, and will doubtlessly continue to do so for centuries to come. It lives and thrives because it adapts to a changing environment, especially in the world of fashion, where over recent decades spinners like Patons have led the way in designs produced for knitters. Mary Thomas wrote in her authoritative *Knitting Book* on the techniques of the craft 'If all the looms in the world ceased to produce cloth, and the art of spinning and knitting alone remained, we could still be clothed, both warmly and fashionably. Such is knitting, which without doubt is the most resourceful and inventive method of fabric construction in the world, being made without loom or machine, without warp or weft, shaped as it is constructed, patterned as whim requires, and divided without being cut'.

The Word Knitting?

The word 'knit' has become firmly rooted in the English language, and is used expressively in fields other than craft work. In the medical world, for example, bones 'knit together'; similarly, in agriculture, hedges 'knit together' and in sociological terms we speak of 'close knit communities'. The use of the word knitting to make a textile fabric – the interlacing of a single thread into a series of loops – was the last use of the word which has entered the common usage as a term for joining or uniting in a much wider sense. Its direct root is in the Anglo-Saxon words, bringing in the notion of knotting, *Cnyttan* which means to knot, and *Cnotta* a knot.

Legends

A legend from ancient mythology may throw light on the history of knitting. Homer's *Odyssey* tells a story of undying love between Ulysses and Penelope. After departing on a long voyage Ulysses was feared dead. Since it was the Greek custom for a widow to remarry, others asked Penelope for her hand but, constant in her love for her husband, she believed that he would one day return and therefore she resisted any thought of remarriage. She began to make a shroud, telling her ardent suitors that once her task was completed, she would choose one from amongst them. However, she secretly unravelled her day's work by night so as to gain as much time as possible. Penelope's work was the same on both sides, and it would have been easier to produce this by knitting than weaving. Hence the supposition that Penelope's work was knitted rather than woven.

The Origins of the Craft

From documented evidence concerning religious practices and laws, from drawings, sculpture and written records, and also from remains of examples of knitting, it is possible to draw some conclusions about the development of knitting through the ages – although what is surmised about the very early days often cannot be confirmed.

Weaving

Primitive man could observe natural order in his own struggle to survive. He would see how the intertwining branches of trees offered some covering, and that the wind would cause tall grasses to intermesh and have a matting effect. Rushes could be woven together to produce a more protective shelter.

The art of weaving developed and man probably possessed these skills well over ten thousand years ago, whilst examples of the weavers' equipment and cloth have been discovered dating back over six thousand years. Weaving requires two threads to be interlaced at right angles. To do this successfully a frame or loom is necessary. This will have a *warp* running the length of the cloth with the *weft* being thrown across, alternatively above and below the warp threads. By no means a simple process for unsophisticated man to master, yet the art of weaving was developed long before knitting.

Knitting

Knitting, when compared to weaving, appears a relatively simple skill to learn. However, it was not until about two thousand years ago that knitted type fabrics, produced using a single, eyed, needle, (not true knitting as known today) developed. Even then there is no evidence of samples of these fabrics until some seventeen hundred years ago.

An Ancient Craft

Some two hundred and fifty years before Jesus Christ, on the borders of ancient Palestine, a fortress was founded by soldiers under the command of Alexander the Great on the banks of the river Euphrates. This in time became the city of Dura Europas and because of its position it gradually developed into a major trading centre. Because of its commercial significance, it frequently changed masters, as conquering armies, including the Romans, set their sights on it. Some five hundred years after it was founded, Dura Europas was completely destroyed by the Persians, and the city soon became buried under the desert sands. Some textile fabrics which resemble knitting were buried and were perfectly preserved in the dry and airless conditions. These were later excavated by a team from Yale University; amongst them were small pieces of fabric almost certainly produced using a single, eyed, needle as the method of their shaping is difficult to achieve with knitting needles. These samples must date back to at least 256 AD, when the city of Dura Europas was destroyed – a date determined precisely because coins found on the site bore this date. The pieces of woollen fabric are too small to ascertain whether they were remains of garments or something else and as they are formed using a crossed Eastern stitch it cannot be said that they were definitely made by true knitting. Two pieces are in ribbing, and the other has had an embossed stitch pattern incorporated in it. Dura Europas was at the crossroads of caravan routes, and these may have been made elsewhere and bartered in the city rather than made by local inhabitants. Nevertheless, they confirm that knitted type fabrics were produced at that time or before.

Other finds sometimes attributed as early knitting (doubtful if they are true knitting), include examples found in Egyptian tombs. These include sandal socks, one of which has been produced in thick brown wool. These are almost perfectly preserved and dated between the fourth and fifth centuries AD. By that time most of the country had become Christian, but the Coptic or early Christians continued the old Egyptian practice of burying personal articles with the dead; these socks were preserved in this way. Then the techniques of making them had developed sufficiently to enable the socks to be made to fit, both by a form of 'turning' the heel and by fashioning the socks. The toes were finished by using a thread of yarn to gather the loops, and there was a cord to draw in the top of the selvedge. Other knitted type items of about the same period found in Egyptian tombs include anklet socks and a doll's cap. Many such exhibits are now held by the Victoria and Albert Museum in London.

Side Winds

As well as the knitting with which people are familiar today, there are a number of ways of interlooping yarn which produce what could be called semi-knit fabrics. For example, as the slip knots of knitting are the sort that ancient trappers used, one source suggests that knitting was started by nomadic hunters. Again, one of the talismans of the ancient Egyptians had a shape similar to the cat's cradle which children make today fingerlooping string; this could have led to a form of semi-knit fabric.

On the eastern shore of the Pacific examples of what has been termed Peruvian needle knitting have been found, dating back to about 100 AD. The Peruvian Indians used a needle similar to today's darning needle and a single thread, and the fabric was produced by securing the thread, taut, and making a first series of loops across this. Then, using a method similar to modern

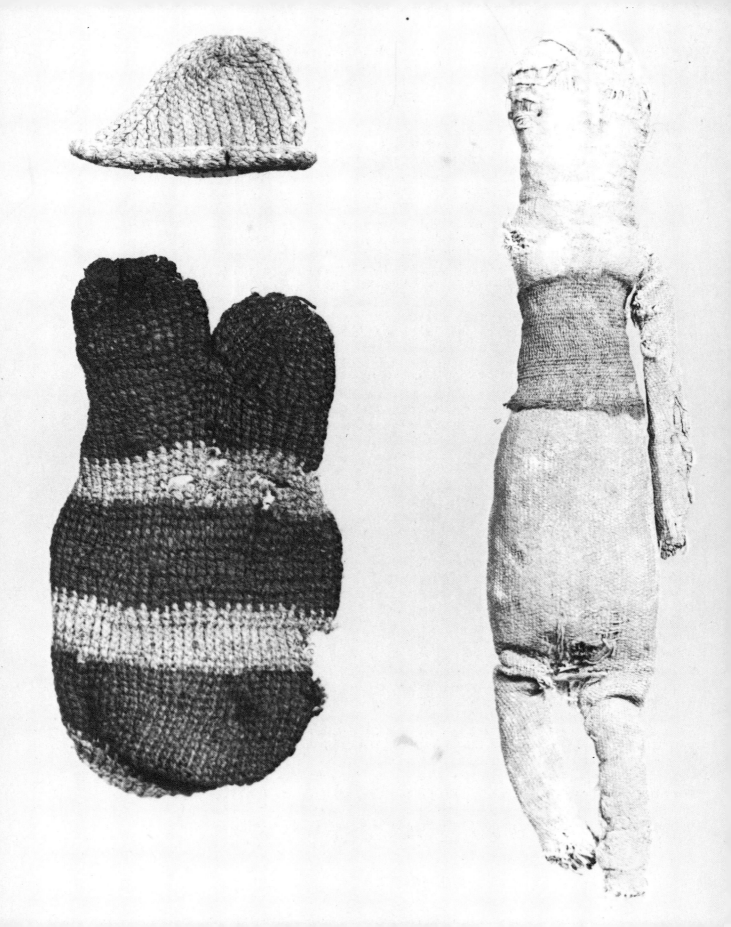

grafting, row upon row of loops were built up until the fabric was the required size. A tedious business, yet it produced a fabric that is indistinguishable from stocking stitch. An example of this is to be found in the Textile Museum in Washington. However, one writer claims that this could have been produced by the technique known as sprang.

Sprang produces a fabric closely resembling knitting except for the fact that the loops are interlocked vertically rather than horizontally. Research into sprang caused a reappraisal of some fabrics labelled by curators in certain museums as knitting, with the result that some exhibits have been re-classified as sprang. Sprang seems to have had a separate yet more or less simultaneous origin in the Scandinavian area and the Middle East, although it also appears to have been taken to, or developed in, the Americas.

Sprang fabrics can be made in a variety of ways. One method of producing it, a form of *needle* sprang, is by setting up fine parallel yarns on a frame, to form the warp which runs vertically. Then, using a thicker yarn, a chain stitch is worked up the first warp thread, and another row of the chain stitch is interlaced into the side loops of the previous row, and so on until the warp has been covered. The warp yarn is then pulled out and a fabric which is something like stocking stitch will have been made. Needle sprang can also be produced without a warp yarn by linking the loops of a single yarn into each other in a similar, but less complex, method as that used in Peruvian needle knitting. In this, the yarn is simply threaded through the adjacent set of loops.

Another method is *plaited* sprang. The yarn that is to produce the final fabric is set up in parallel rows on the frame and then these are interlinked, using a form of plaiting with two sticks which are moved onwards to hold each section of the fabric made in place. When all the threads have been dealt with the yarn is secured and the sticks removed. Basic sprang fabric would be ornamented, sometimes using elaborate embroidery.

Early Frame Knitting

Before the invention of the mechanical knitting machine in the sixteenth century, a crude form of knitting frame had been in use for probably as long as knitting on needles had been carried out. The ancient Arabs, who had weaving frames long before the birth of Christ, and who were probably the originators of handknitting, may also have developed a primitive form of knitting frame.

Today, young children are taught to make a simple cord by winding yarn round four or so nails which have been hammered into a cotton reel and, using a crochet hook, loop stitches over one another to produce a cord. This could have been the basis of the early Arab knitting frames.

The Spread of Knitting

The founders of the primitive Church, in their early missionary visits to the Arab world, where many converts were to be made, would have seen, and possibly copied, the craft from the Arabs. The spread of Christianity was followed by those with a more secular interest – the Coptic traders. They moved around in the Mediterranean, to Asia and the coast of Africa and may have seen the knitted Coptic caps worked in diverse patterned designs and perhaps carried them from Egypt along the Mediterranean shores into Spain. Knitting may then have reached northern Italy from Spain. And from Spain it would have been but a small step to France, Germany and the Netherlands.

Doll's cap, knitted in light brown wool, c.500 A.D. Found in Egyptian tomb at Bahnasa.

"Lady from the Island of Mykonos" by the Baron of Stackelberg.

Not too far away, England was becoming a Christian country. Traders would be taking knitted goods to the developing ports in the south-west and increasingly to London. From these places coastal traders could have taken samples of the craft and their skills up the east coast and into Scotland.

Melton Grass in his *History of Hosiery* writes 'When the Arabs conquered Egypt in 641 AD, they founded a flourishing textile industry. Both native Mohammedans and the Copts were willing to continue their weaving and knitting for their new masters... By the 8th century the old Iberian culture was absorbed by the Islamic culture and there are now two hypotheses as to how the art of handknitting was introduced to Europe. One is that the families of the troops and the traders who followed them, practised the art in the new homeland and taught it to the natives... The other hypothesis gives credit to the primitive Christian Church. It is known that Coptic missionaries were sent on journeys to Spain and Italy. It is believed that having produced the art of knitting in Egypt, the missionaries brought this knowledge with them to Europe.'

It seems that when knitters moved away from using bones as knitting implements to more sophisticated tools, needles with hooks (somewhat like crochet hooks) were developed. These were used in Asia Minor and also in areas where the Spanish influence was strong such as the Landes in Southern France, the Basque district of Spain and in parts of South America, though they are being used by fewer knitters today and there is danger of their use dying out.

It should of course be remembered that man as well as woman was an exponent of knitting in its early days. The soldiers, shepherds and fishermen were the overland and sea travellers of the time and many of them would have been competent, skilful and prodigious knitters. Knitting skills would have travelled with them, especially as they tended to take their women with them wherever they went. By the Middle Ages knitting had spread from its home in Asia Minor all over Europe, and in the other direction to Central Asia. However, it was not until the growth of European colonialism and expanding empires that knitting reached other parts of the globe.

CHAPTER 2
Knitting, Religion and the Guilds

There are many interesting tales connected with the development of knitting in Europe.

Throughout the Middle Ages religion was supreme. The Church provided what little education and training was to be had in those times, and it was a major patron of the arts, even if this patronage only embraced art forms of which the Church approved. The design, adornment and maintenance of places of worship was a manifestation of man's desire to create beautiful edifices as well as a means of worshipping God. The Church as patron has left a rich heritage to enjoy, and without the legacy of its sponsorship our lives today would all be much the poorer.

The modern distinction between the artist and the craftsman was less sharply defined in times past, and many artisans were both. Craftsmen of the period produced an essentially practical product; embellishment may have been a secondary objective, yet it would have given the opportunity to demonstrate artistic skills.

Man – The Knitter
In eary history, man took the role of shepherd, partly because of the danger involved with wild animals roaming in a largely untamed environment. Later, as the countryside became more widely inhabited and cultivated, and wild animals were driven further afield, shepherding could be left to boys. Similarly, fishing required a certain physical robustness, and the seas were dangerous, so fishing became a man's burden.

Both tending flocks of sheep and waiting for a catch involve long periods of inactivity – often tedious, frequently quite alone. Time then may seem to have been less precious than today, with life proceeding at a more leisurely pace, but this was not so. All work had to be carried out by hand at the appropriate time, according to season, or weather, or light with a constant risk of starvation if the harvest failed. Shepherds and fishermen utilised their time not spent tending the flock or taking in the catch in other useful employ, such as collecting clumps of wool that had been snagged on bushes, or mending nets. Naturally any such tasks could not involve much in the way of equipment. Knitting fitted the bill exactly.

So, although knitting was not entirely a male preserve and women did indeed practise the craft, men were the major partner in the production of knitted fabrics and garments in years gone by. Sometimes shepherds, after

A rare painting of knitting in practice. An abbey altar-piece known as *'The Visit of the Angels'*, by Meiister Bertram, painted between 1390 and 1400. The knitter is the Virgin Mary.

1070. — Jeunes Filles de Pontivy

gathering wool, would 'spin' it with their fingers ready for knitting up. This is illustrated in the unusual picture of the Landes shepherd.

Women, working in the homestead, began more and more to take on the job of spinning wool, producing yarns from animal fibres, usually wool, or of vegetable fibres, such as flax. The menfolk would then take this yarn and needles away from the home base to their work place where they would knit it up.

Even as late as the nineteenth century, the men of the Yorkshire Dales were famed for their prolific knitting, although by that time knitting had become an irrevocably female preserve.

Religion

One of the classic paintings associated with handknitting is the celebrated picture by Meister Bertram. Dating from about 1390-1400, and entitled *Der Besuch des Engels* (The Visit of the Angels), it features the Virgin Mary knitting in the round, which led to its popular name of *The Knitting Madonna*.

The Master Knitters designed and created beautiful, often elaborate, gloves for the clergy to wear. The higher up the ecclesiastical order, the more ornate the design would be. As yet no evidence has been found to confirm that knitting was carried out within monasteries and convents.

Early historical records in Europe, which were maintained by clerics, frequently concern the nobility and royalty. The few references to knitted goods between the fifteenth and seventeenth centuries tend to reflect the activity of the well-to-do. Records suggest that outer garments such as caps,

Shepherd with stilt-seat watching his flock (Landes, Southwestern France)

The shepherds of the Landes in Southern France wear the strangest "professional" garbs while tending their flocks. In order to oversee his large herd and watch the stragglers, the shepherd moved about on stilts about six feet long. A third support made a tripod out of the biped when he wanted to rest. Dressed in sheepskin, the shepherd whiled away the dull moments, most appropriately, by knitting woollen socks.

17

gloves, hose and shirts were knitted extensively throughout Europe, and even some undergarments were knitted. One writer suggests that the technique for handknitting gloves goes back at least as far as the thirteenth century in Italy, as it is believed that Pope Innocent IV wore gloves knitted in silk. In the sixteenth century sumptuary laws – laws prohibiting excessive displays of wealth – were passed in Germany forbidding commoners to wear silk stockings although they were permitted to don woollen ones. This legislation even restricted royalty to wearing silk stockings only on a Sunday, the rationale being that silk stockings had to be imported from Spain or Italy, and the law would protect the home wool trade. When Henri II of France was married to Catherine de Medici in 1533 in Venice it is said that he wore handknitted silk stockings. In France, hosiery knitting had by that time become an important industry in several parts of the country.

Although many guilds of handknitters were established in a number of European countries, and guilds for other crafts and trades were established in the British Isles, there are no records of knitting guilds in England at that time.

Knitting in England

It is not certain how knitting came to the British Isles. One possibility is that soldiers fighting in France and Spain learned the skill there and brought it home with them; the craft could have been established in these shores by the fifteenth century. No doubt the history of knitting in Britain goes back even further. It is suggested that as early as the fourteenth century ceremonial gloves were being knitted in countries such as Spain. It is claimed that the gloves kept at New College Oxford were worn by William of Wykenham, Bishop of Winchester, when performing the opening ceremony of the college in 1386. However it is more likely that these are of a later date and possibly belonged to Warham, the Archbishop of Canterbury, in the sixteenth century. In addition, in the records of the Church of Saints Peter and Wilfred, in Ripon, Yorkshire, for the period covering 1452 to 1456, there is an entry in a will concerning a 'knyt gyrdyll' although this possibly refers to a knotted one.

References to hose or stockings abound for this period. Long before records of handknitting were found men wore hose. These were originally made from woven cloth which was cut and sewn to shape. It appears that the actual yarn used to make the hose would sometimes depend upon the rank or status of the person wearing them, so this might have ranged from a rough cotton or coarse wool to linen or silk, depending upon what they could afford. Such cut and sewn hose, although fitting like today's jeans, had little elasticity, and when stockings made by handknitting were produced, they had great appeal because of their better comfort. Stockings would be knitted in cotton or worsted. The date of their appearance has been put at 1564. Gravenor Henson writes in his *History of the Framework-Knitters* 'Knit stockings were first introduced into England from Mantua, in Italy. William Rider, a clothier ... being at the house of an Italian merchant ... saw a pair of knit stockings and had the ingenuity to make a pair exactly like them, which he presented to Sir William Herbert, then Earl of Pembroke'. Thus he was said to have introduced the style into England.

England also had its sumptuary laws to regulate expenditure on knitted items. In 1488, in the reign of Henry VII, an Act was passed which laid down the price of knitted woollen caps as two shillings and eight pence (14p).

Probably the most famous of the Engish sumptuary laws concerning knitting was the Cappers Act of 1571. This stipulated that on Sundays and

Holy Days everyone above the age of six years had to wear a knitted cap made by an English capper. Exceptions were made for those travelling, and ladies and gentlemen, knights, lords and the rich. There was a fine of three shillings and four pence (17p) for non-compliance with this order, which was enacted to provide a protected market not only for cappers but also for the English wool trade. The reign of Elizabeth I also saw an Act, the Statute of Servants, which restricted the cost of hosiery worn by servants to three shillings (15p) a pair. Henry VIII claimed that he wore fine knitted stockings from Paris where the knitters of the day were said to have had the edge over English craftsmen. During Elizabeth's reign, the more delicate stockings which were being produced in Spain grew in popularity, despite the rivalry of the two countries. Elizabeth's father, Henry VIII, had worn Spanish hose and the merchant and financier Sir Thomas Gresham had presented a pair of Spanish stockings to Edward VI. But it was Elizabeth, enjoying her title of Gloriana, who created a fashionable English Court and introduced many new styles to England. In 1560 it is said that the Queen's silkwoman, a Mrs Montague, knitted a pair of fine stockings in black silk for Elizabeth, who was so delighted with their comfort and delicate appearance that she vowed she would never wear cloth ones again. A later major mention of royalty and knitting concerns Charles I. When imprisoned by Oliver Cromwell and the Roundheads he had a beautifully knitted silk shirt. This demonstrated the excellence of the craftsmanship of the Master Knitter, probably Italian, who made it. It was knitted in the round, and has a superb texture created by the geometrical construction of its stitch patterning. It is suggested that when the King was executed in 1649 he may have been wearing this shirt, which can be seen at the London Museum.

The Guilds

By the late sixteenth century handknitting had become quite widespread in Europe, and provided income for the artisan knitters. It was also carried out as a pastime by the upper and middle classes on a small scale, amongst whom other needlecrafts were popular as well, with embroidery and tapestry work being thought especially fitting for gentlefolk. The most interesting examples of knitting which survive today are knitted carpets or wall hangings, created by the masters of the craft, although none of these is English. They survived largely because they were commissioned for their aesthetic value and were hung to adorn the walls of castles or manor houses rather than being used as expensive draught excluders. These were produced mainly during the sixteenth and seventeenth centuries in all the major knitting centres throughout Europe except apparently those in the British Isles. This was the period when the craft had been brought to its height by the Master Knitters.

The guilds set up in the Middle Ages were the equivalent of an employers' association and trade union, rolled into one. Their objectives were to maintain the quality of the goods produced to protect the consumers, and to protect their own members. The lengthy apprenticeship, although ensuring a high level of competence, also had the effect of limiting the number of members. The guild could also regulate price, to help protect the income level of its members. Guilds in many European countries date back to the twelfth century.

By the fifteenth century, knitting had become one of the staple industries of France and so it is perhaps not surprising that it is believed that the first guild specifically for knitters was founded in Paris in 1527. This guild, like many others, had a patron saint. However, although St. Fiacre was technically the patron saint of the Paris Guild of Knitters, some writers claim that he is the patron saint of knitters in general. St. Fiacre was undoubtedly popular in Paris, where he also gave his name to the fiacre, the small pony cart that was used in the city. He is also the patron saint of gardeners. Some sources suggest that he was the son of a Scottish King, although St. Fiacre was more likely to have been of Irish origin; his remains are at Meaux in France.

Guilds of knitters were soon to spring up in many places in Europe following the formation of the one in Paris. A guild of knitters was founded in Strasbourg in 1535, and in Prague in 1570 the knitters split off from the guild of clothiers to form their own guild. Records suggest that by the second half of the sixteenth century, guilds of knitters in Alsace, Bohemia, Leipzig, Frankfurt, Hamburg and Vienna were well developed. Whilst in England there appear to have been no guilds of handknitters, there are references to members of other guilds being involved in handknitting – for example, the cappers and the haberdashers. It appears that guilds were also to be found in the major provincial cities such as Bristol, Chester and Norwich, as well as London.

The Masterwork

The statutes of some of the European knitters' guilds required that before membership could be conferred, a masterwork had to be produced, and the quality of some of these works is awesome. These were made by the knitting craft apprentices to show how well they had learned and developed their skills.

The Master Knitters – almost exclusively men, although it is recorded that in some guilds if a member died his wife could take his place – had a jealously guarded reputation to maintain. They made great demands upon the creative ability of their apprentices, stretching both their intelligence and knitting skills to the limit over the three years it took to learn the craft, the final test lasting over a thirteen week period. The masterpiece would often be a knitted carpet, but might also have been beautifully patterned ecclesiastical gloves, or an elaborately styled waistcoat in silk. As well as knitting the masterpiece, the apprentice was required to produce additional items – a knitted shirt, a felted beret, hose using a turned heel, or whatever was laid down by the local guild.

The knitted carpet was chosen so often as the masterpiece for it offered scope for examining both creativity and technical ability. It had to be an original design, submitted for acceptance before the knitting began. Most designs were bible pictures. Yet it could echo nature, being built up of intricate foliage patterns incorporating flowers and trees, perhaps with birds and animals as well. Sometimes the insignia or coat of arms associated with a sponsor would be worked into the design, and a name or date. The design could require up to twenty different colours. The size of these projects was often staggering, the most common being about 2.4 metres square.

Distinctive colour stitch-patterns can be made relatively easily in stocking stitch using two needles. However, for the larger carpets, these needles would have had to be over two metres long! So it would appear that a number of shorter needles would have had to be used. Some kind of frame would have been needed to support the weight of the work in progress. This work would have taken the apprentice around two months to complete. Finishing might have required a primitive form of fulling, by soaking the carpet and then stamping or beating it. On some garments the fibres would be raised with a teasel and any unevenness on the surface trimmed off with scissors.

Knitted carpet, Alsace

Once his masterpiece had been accepted, the apprentice had crossed the first hurdle to his becoming a Master Craftsman. Usually he would spend the next three years as a journeyman knitter, perhaps travelling out of his own locality or even to another country to learn other techniques and skills. Hired by the day, all the while learning and perhaps having to perform other tasks to earn his keep, he eventually gained enough experience to join a guild.

21

An Established Industry

By the fifteenth and sixteenth centuries, knitting had become an established industry in most of Europe, albeit a cottage one. It was an industry that produced basic goods for the masses, but also finery for the upper classes of the day. And although the English industry does not appear to have been as well organised as its continental counterparts, nevertheless it had its own dynamism. In Elizabethan England knitting schools were set up to teach the 'arte and misterie' of handknitting to children and adolescents. An excellent reputation was held by one such school in Nottingham which attracted students from all over England. The Poor Laws of the Tudor period encouraged the setting up of these schools – requirements were few – simple implements and basic yarns.

In Norfolk, poor children were put into knitting and spinning schools, and if parents were unable to pay the fees demanded, then churchwardens were obliged to do so. In Norwich itself, an order was passed requiring every parish to provide a knitting-school dame to teach the craft to the poor, whether child or adult, in order to train them for some future employment. Queen Elizabeth I visited the city in 1578 and was captivated at a celebratory pageant by a tableau consisting of eight small girls spinning yarns on one side and eight small girls knitting stockings on the other. Some of the basic knitting produced during the Tudor period was indeed the result of child labour. But the reputation of English knitting was growing, and England was exporting knitted goods to Europe. At Rouen in France, knitters were making stockings of an "English" design, and English stockings were held in great esteem.

By the end of the Middle Ages, knitting was firmly established as an industry both in England and abroad.

CHAPTER 3
European Traditions Develop

By the sixteenth century, knitting had become well established in Europe. Although the cradle of the craft had originally been in the Middle East, around the Mediterranean, it never appeared to reach the art form which it was to find in the Europe of the post-Renaissance period.

Although winter nights can be cold in the Eastern Mediterranean area, the climate, dust and sand of the region are not conducive to the production of finely knitted fabrics. So it would appear to have been left to later Europeans to stretch the possibilities of the craft; with hindsight it can be argued that the prevailing conditions in Renaissance Europe favoured this development.

Of course, stitch patterns would travel. They would be taken to the various corners of continental Europe, and thence to all parts of the globe, by travellers and traders. People on journeys would have carried or worn all sorts of symbols associated with their civilisation or culture – symbols based on geometrical shapes and signs, symbols that might frequently have a religious theme or represent the wearer's status. The explorers, warriors, evangelists and traders would introduce these to an area where they might be copied. Knitters were not the first to assimilate these designs into their craft, but in time they would have adopted them. The reason that a symbol or sign was used would pass into folklore, explained by word of mouth, or even be lost in antiquity.

Many stitch patterns can be found in diverse locations; for example, the bobbles and diamonds of German knitting are also to be found in Aran designs. Cable, so popular with fishing communities, has travelled to the sweaters worn on England's cricket fields. Heinz Edgar Kiewe writes that in the 1930s 'there was only one interlace pattern in the vocabulary of the British knitter and that was the cable-stich used exclusively on the Jersey-Guernsey Isle by fishermen and for those 'cricket sweaters' one of the earliest of handknitted folk designs and common to the English village greens of Victorian days'.

Weather, customs and fashions over the centuries have all combined to affect the style of dress, and knitting has become inextricably bound into these.

Knitting traditions tended to develop along two major routes. Firstly there was the splendour of the items made by the Master Knitters, frequently produced for the nobility or the rich. These used intricate stitch and colour patterns, sometimes further embellished by embroidery. This required a very high standard of draughtsmanship in the design of knitted fabrics, as well as the ability to knit skilfully the fine yarns used to make them and knowledge of the properties of yarns and the combination of colour. When he commissioned the spinning and dyeing of yarns from other crafts, he had to be exact in his specifications.

On a more humble and workaday level, there was the development of folk knitting. This frequently lay somewhere between being a hobby and a local industry, and was mainly engaged in producing utilitarian goods, generally for protection against the weather. Although thicker, coarser yarns were knitted and colours were often drab, the patterns produced were interesting, sometimes elaborate, and peasant knitting frequently developed a distinctive art of its own.

Recording these traditions is a difficult matter. To use categories such as social class, nationality or even pattern-groupings, will fail to show the whole picture particularly as handknitting has undergone a change from being an industry to a hobby. An effective approach may be to highlight some national features. It is important to remember that traditions are not laid down according to national frontiers and may significantly overlap.

Austria and Germany
Embossing and Embellishing
The cold temperatures and mountainous regions of the Austrian Tyrol and German states provide a severe environment. Knitting traditions for garments based on knotted and heavy cabled fabrics knitted in natural wool were developed. When plain fabrics were produced, even those with a heavily patterned one-coloured stitch, these would be decorated by embroidering patterns on top of them using brightly coloured yarns. The stitch-patterns from these areas could be based upon cable stitches interwoven in narrow panels, frequently twisting the panels over the whole area of the knitting, or upon a plaited stitch-pattern together with relief stitches. The cables would twist a number of stitches, whereas the plaited patterns would often only move one stitch at a time, which made them much quicker to produce, yet just as impressive. Where vertical stitch panels were knitted to provide a high relief effect, some all-over pattern which had less emphasis on the relief would be knitted on either side. Bobbles which were knitted into the fabric also became an important feature. The garments produced included waistcoats, knitted using embossed stitch-patterns, which were prime examples of garments that incorporated heavy and colourful embroidery.

The man's knitted stocking is probably the most notable knitted item from the area. By the eighteenth century, it had become part of the national costume. Unlike stockings from further east, these were made in a cream-coloured yarn with the emphasis on the heavy stitch-patterning. They tended to be left as they had been knitted, without the flourish of embroidery. Women also wore cream knitted stockings, or leg warmers, made in stocking stitch. The special feature of the leg warmers was the horizontal pleating achieved by making them much longer than the normal leg length, and then folding them concertina-fashion to give the pleated effect required.

In the 1970s there was a craze in knitting for bomber jackets, a feature of which was a looped stitch which gave an interesting surface texture as well as providing added warmth to the garment. Although not exactly the same, it does emphasise the point that in knitting, as elsewhere, nothing is new. For in the Austrian mountains girls would wear hats which had been made with an outer 'shell' formed with a looped stitch and a folded-in lining. The peasants of the time in some Austrian village can be imagined, the man in his beautifully embossed hand-knitted waistcoat and cream stockings, the woman in her hand-knitted cap and leg warmers. The couple kept just that little bit warmer because of these knitted garments.

Belgium
Lace
Although lace knitting was carried out in many parts of Europe (the Shetland island of Unst becoming particularly famous for it), because of the long tradition of lace-making in Belgium it was inevitable that knitters would reproduce lace-like patterns in their handknitting. Fine wool or gossamer-thin silk would be used to produce shawls, doilies and the like, using intricate lace stitches.

Eastern Europe
Peasant Socks
The tradition of peasant socks was one of the major knitting traditions to develop in a number of countries but especially so in Eastern Europe. They added colour to the local costumes worn at festivities and gave warmth in these colder zones of the continent. In a later section on Scandinavia it will be seen that this art form spread its wings.

The colourful classic form of the peasant sock comes from the Balkans where these were made from a multiplicity of techniques including knitting. Hardwearing examples of these socks have been found which were produced using multi-coloured coarse wool, worn over thinner socks made of a softer textured wool. An example of such, from Albania dating back to the nineteenth century, is to be found in the Victoria and Albert Museum in London. The strong and contrasting colouring of the yarns is the major feature of these socks and makes the final product unique to the area. The effect came about because the colour-pattern combination of light yarns on dark, and vice versa, was put together in patterns of horizontals, verticals and diagonals. Whilst the design of the stitch-pattern frequently includes many sophisticated combinations, the shaping of the sock has been reduced to simplicity itself.

France
Silk Hose and Peasant 'Brioche'
Knitting came to France from Spain and by the sixteenth century had become a major industry. The Spanish influence, and the demands of royalty and the court, dictated that finely knitted garments should be produced by the country's Master Knitters. It seems that Henri II was the originator of the fashion for silk stockings when he wore a pair at his wedding in 1533. Other monarchs in Europe soon followed this trend, reaping the benefits not only of comfort and better fit, but also the undoubted status which these superbly produced hose bestowed.

The peasants of France also developed their own traditions in knitting, especially in the colder, northern districts of the country. Called 'brioche' knitting elsewhere, the French referred to it as 'English stitch'. It is based on a single coloured yarn, but with distinctive stitch patterns. The brioche stitch is formed by knitting into the centre of the stitch under that which is normally knitted, so knitting the two stitches together. The basic brioche stitch is used

for ribbing, moss and many other variations.

The influence of the Basque districts on peasant knitting is considerable, with patterns having a natural base but using bright colours to incorporate designs both from nature and mythology.

Holland
Embossed Knitting

Embossed knitting was to be found all over Europe, but examples from Holland indicate that this form of knitting had been developed to the form of an art by the eighteenth century. The fabric was knitted in a fine yarn in a stocking stitch background at an extremely close tension of up to nine stitches and fourteen rows to the centimetre. The embossing was formed using plain and purl stitches. Patterns incorporated animals, birds and trees, not in a systematic or symmetrical design but rather to enhance the picture by following the randomness of nature. Great skill and patience would be necessary to produce such intricate knitting.

Italy
Silk Knitting from Florence

The craft of fine knitting appears to have spread from Spain to Italy, where the art of knitting in fine silks, using rich colours, was perfected to make exquisite coats which were fastened by many tiny buttons. This tradition of knitting reached a height of excellence in Renaissance Florence. The basic method of making these elaborately patterned designs lay in the knitting of proportioned panels. Embroidery would often be used to highlight the main features of the patterning. Sleeveless coats – waistcoats – were made, and ornate caps were fashionable for both men and women.

The tradition of these garments has been carried down into contemporary Italian knitting. Although the materials used, and the patterns employed then were no doubt different, the reputation of today's Italian knitwear is still just as high.

Scandinavia

Denmark, Norway and Sweden have a long and fine tradition of knitting to their credit. In the sixteenth century the King of Denmark was presented with a pair of fully fashioned silk knitted hose which were made in Holland. He was so impressed with these that he encouraged Dutch knitters to come to Denmark and teach his subjects to knit.

James Norbury, sometime Chief Designer for Patons & Baldwins Limited, and celebrated for his pioneer studies of the history of the craft, as well as for his knitting designs, relates an amusing tale about the impact of knitting in Denmark. The King, it appears, was very pleased with the new silk stockings but was anxious that they should be restricted to the Court, hence a law was passed permitting only courtiers to wear fine silk hosiery. Almost immediately there was dissension from the townspeople of Copenhagen who objected to their having to wear wrap-round puttees, since even the comparatively crude cut and sewn hose were not then widely available in the country. This pressure led to a second act, stating that the townspeople could wear knitted hose, but stipulating that these must be made from cotton, not in silk as worn by the King and members of the Court. In turn, this led the peasants to take up the cry; why should their urban brothers have the advantage of wearing closely fitted knitted hose when they had only their puttees? So a third act was

Woollen peasant socks, Albania, 19th Century.

Girls knitting – Zeeland, Holland

Cap of knitted silk. Italian. 17th Century.

passed stating that they could wear hose, but these had to be of coarse wool! James Norbury concludes this story by suggesting that in those days you could tell the social class of a Dane by looking at what he was wearing on his legs.

The bitter weather of the region ensured that knitting would soon take hold, and the craft quickly spread to Finland, the Faeroes, Greenland and Iceland. Jumpers, hats, scarves, mittens, leg warmers and stockings were all necessities. Even when knitted in thick coarse yarns, people still wanted to embellish them. This was usually done by making the garments multi-coloured. Although the patterns employed the symmetrical designs which are now well associated with the area, each country developed quite distinctive uses of colour and geometrical patterning. Whereas knitters in the other Nordic countries tended to use Fair Isle-style colourings, Norwegians frequently used white yarns to help contrast in patterned effects. Shapes also differed, with the Swedes in general emphasising a square-shaped neck, and Icelanders preferring jerseys which were loosely knitted.

The Russian Steppes

From south-western Europe knitting passed through the Central European plains towards the east. It appears that a Russian handknitting trade developed, based in the Moscow area and influenced by countries such as

Knitted hat reputedly bought in Holland by Peter I.

Spain and Holland producing items for both the military and the Church although Russian knitting never reached the standards set by knitters in Western Europe. It is suggested that Peter I had a felted cap brought from Holland. The sword sashes worn by officers were often knitted and served another useful purpose; having been made from a strong yarn, they could be slipped over two poles to make a stretcher. The hoods worn by priests were also knitted. These, referred to as *klobuki*, were sometimes decorated by embroidering, for example, the symbol of the Holy Spirit – the bird with the human face – onto the cap.

Spain and the Basque Country

It would seem that Spain was the womb of European knitting. Early Spanish knitting has found echoes in France, Italy and England amongst others, and a quirk of politics and weather combined to take Spaniards as far north as Fair Isle where they are said to have influenced the knitting which has retained its strength as a traditional skill.

In the warmer areas of the European continent the accent was on fine knitting. The early and beautifully made knitted gloves show how the art of knitting became well developed in Spain. Apart from the fine and expensive yarns which went into the making of ceremonial altar gloves, the high standards that the craft had reached by the fifteenth century are also evident.

"Klobuk" headdress. 17th Century.

Knitted in the round, using silk thread at a very fine tension, the stitch patterning was generally symmetrical. The workmanship would have been conspicuously displayed when these were worn by the bishop, who always removed them before approaching the altar.

In the Basque country, the peasant community developed their own styles of knitting, in which felting played a prominent part. Felting and fulling becoming important techniques in fabric finishing. The classic example of felting was provided in the development of the Basque beret. This was knitted in the round in stocking stitch, using a coarse yarn, to a size some three times as large as eventually required by the wearer. After the knitting the beret was immersed and left to soak in water, and later pummelled with heavy stones to cause it to felt. Once at the size required, the beret was fitted over a large round stone of appropriate size and left to set to shape as it dried. Felted knitting developed and played an important part in knitted fashions in the sixteenth- and seventeenth-centuries and was used in the production of Tudor caps and Scottish knitted bonnets.

Switzerland
Beads and Bedspreads

Beaded knitting was not the sole prerogative of the Swiss, for examples of this form of knitting are to be found in many countries. It became the fashion at one time in Victorian England, created substantial interest in France and

Knitted bedspread – Stranger's Hall Museum, Norwich.

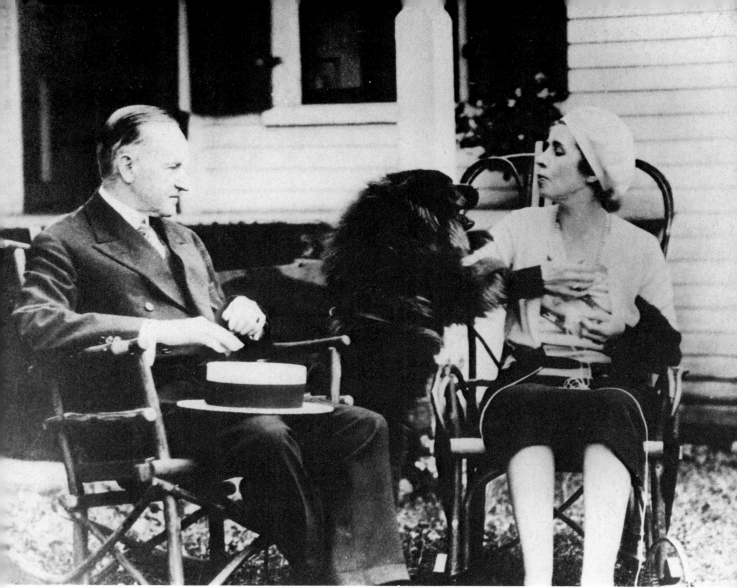

President and Mrs Coolidge with Red Chow in front of Coolidge Homestead at Plymouth Notch, Vermont, c.1924 (Mrs Coolidge knitting).

Germany and even travelled to the United States of America. However, perhaps it is especially appropriate to associate beaded knitting with the Swiss. Intricate to make, with the beads threaded on the yarn, it requires the same application and precision which is associated with the Swiss watchmaker.

Technically, beads can be incorporated in knitting in two ways. Firstly, there is 'beaded knitting' where beads are used more or less to cover the fabric and to form the pattern. The knitter has to have the patience to thread numerous beads, often of different colours, onto the yarn before knitting with it. Secondly, for the garment which is not to look too pretentious but where a stitch pattern needs to be highlighted, the knitter can 'knit with beads'. In this it is the yarn which makes the stitch-pattern, and this may be coloured or plain, while the beads, which may be of one colour, are simply used for emphasis. In the United States of America in the nineteenth century, knitted bead bags were in vogue, and were produced by skilled craftswomen who could earn up to five dollars for making a bag. The designs on these varied, sometimes featuring figures or landscapes, and they became a much admired

John Paton, founder of John Paton, Son & Co., Ltd.

33

and treasured possession. Brides, who had commissioned them to complement the wedding dress, might carry one to their wedding.

The Swiss also developed the art of knitting superb bedspreads using cotton yarns. Examples of such work are to be found in many European countries, including a fine collection at the Stranger's Hall Museum, Norwich. These items, which do not lend themselves to being knitted in wool, started to appear in the eighteenth century when the spinning and bleaching of cotton yarn was improved. Bedspreads became the nineteenth-century equivalent of the seventeenth-century knitted masterpiece, the knitted carpet. However, they have an advantage in that they can be knitted in small panels or strips before final asembly. This approach to their knitting also enables panels to be repeated all over the final bedspread, or varied and made up in some symmetrical order to produce a most attractive finished article. This example of the development of the craft was also found in the United States of America. For example Grace Coolidge, the wife of President Calvin Coolidge (1923-1929) had a grandmother who knitted a superb bedspread, featuring a raised leaf pattern. It was said of Mrs Coolidge herself that she was never without some knitting, and there is a portrait of her sitting on a sofa in the White House which depicts her with a bundle of knitting by her side.

It can be seen that with its many varying traditions, knitting was firmly established in Renaissance Europe, but its continued existence was soon to be seriously threatened.

CHAPTER 4
A Cloud On The Horizon

The rumblings of activity which culminated in the Industrial Revolution of the late eighteenth and early nineteenth centuries could be heard as far back as the Elizabethan Age.

In the thirteenth century the development of mechanical fulling mills was probably the first step in the industrialisation of the textile industry. In Elizabeth's reign there was the so-called Nef's Industrial Revolution, mainly based on the advances in coal production. Other minor inventions were developed during the centuries preceding the Industrial Revolution proper, and of these, the forerunner of today's industrial and domestic knitting machines was all-important to this story of knitting, and proved a watershed in the history of the craft.

Before the stocking frame was introduced, handknitting had become an important industry. It provided the knitting craftsmen with their livelihood; it gave added income to peasants in a number of areas and the industry provided clothing. Today, centuries after the invention of the stocking frame, knitting has become a leisure pursuit for many.

The reason is self-evident. Mechanisation sounded the death knell for many of the ancient crafts, with the artisan being made completely superfluous in many cases. Later it will be seen that Queen Elizabeth I was not exactly pleased to learn of the invention of 'an engine to knit', fearing that it would deprive some of her subjects of their very livelihood, which could in turn lead to unrest – a great fear of the Tudors. With hindsight, in the second Elizabethan Age when possibly a greater number of the population can and do ply their needles than in Gloriana's day, we can see that she need not have feared the death of knitting as a craft, but she was right about its future as an industry.

William Lee
The inventor of the stocking frame, and a man before his time, was William Lee. It is supposed that the year he finally perfected his invention was 1589, the year following that of the Spanish Armada.

He was born about 1550, but there are no records as to the exact date in either of the two parishes in which it was claimed he was born, St Swithin's of Woodborough or St Wilfrid's of Calverton in Nottinghamshire.

His university education at Christ's and St John's Colleges, Cambridge, led to ordination in the Church as curate of Calverton. While he was at Calverton, his younger brother James, came to live with him.

The Legends Behind the Invention of the Knitting Machine

Unlike the stories behind the discovery of penicillin or radium, or the invention of the steam engine, there was no 'lucky accident' to point the way. Unlike Archimedes in his bath or Newton sitting under the apple tree, there was no sudden inspiration. Of the possible reasons for the development, two are appealing.

One suggests that William Lee was besotted by a young woman from Nottingham who was engaged in the running of a knitting school. This was a most successful enterprise and she had dedicated her life to its promotion, so much so, that there was little time left for outside interests, least of all for poor William. With all the chagrin that unrequited love can foster, William set about taking his revenge on the one thing that had kept him apart from her — knitting. A machine would effectively render handknitting obsolete. Here, the story goes, the machine he produced was so successful that the knitting school had to be closed and the woman was left dreaming as to what might have been.

Another relates that William was courting a young woman and when he used to visit her she did not put her knitting aside, which he felt to be discourteous, and she ignored his attempts to entertain her. Spurned, and angry that his attentions and affection should thus be repaid by coldness, he determined upon producing a machine that would take away her consuming

William Lee, while watching his wife knit, conceived the idea of imitating the movements of her fingers in a machine.

passion for knitting! In this version the story ends with the girl eventually seeing the light, but by then it is too late as he is already wrapped up in his invention.

The Invention of the Stocking Frame
The stories surrounding the invention are probably more interesting than the facts. The legends suggest either economic necessity or revenge as the motive. It is more likely that William Lee determined upon the machine's development as a challenge. His early background on the farm, his observation of carpenters and smiths at work, the fact that he had watched the women of his family knitting, combined with his educated and enquiring mind, provided the necessary conditions for the invention of the machine. He developed needles which had been tempered and bent to give a hooked end. These were mounted on a frame and, although somewhat different from the latched needle on today's home knitting machine, worked on a similar principle of drawing the yarn through each row of loops to form a new row of stitches. This parallel with today's domestic knitting machine even went as far as the requisite sinkers to weigh the thread down as each new row of stitches was being formed. The completed stocking frame looked a rather cumbersome device and contained over three thousand parts. When William Lee's finally developed version was used by a trained operator to knit up the coarse yarn, which was all that the first machines would take, it could form stitches five or six times as fast as the skilled hand knitter, who it was estimated could knit at a speed of about one hundred stitches a minute.

Queen Elizabeth and the Machine
The machine was taken to London, then a prosperous capital city of some quarter of a million inhabitants. Renting a house at Bunhill Fields, he set up his machine which soon aroused great interest.

In Tudor times, if a patent were granted for some aspect of trade or industry, it would in effect confer monopoly rights on the recipient and could lead to great wealth. Once settled, for success to be assured William Lee needed to obtain letters patent. In his quest for this he required a patron to bring him to the attention of the monarch. Lord Hunsdon, a cousin of the Queen, was persuaded to act on his behalf in this matter. In due course, Queen Elizabeth granted an audience to William Lee by visiting his workshop for a demonstration of the techniques of framework knitting. Despite her reputation for fashion consciousness, and the impression that the two enterprising young subjects, William and his brother James, may have made on her, the Queen could not conceal her disappointment at the rough, woollen stockings which were being produced by the device. Writing dramatically of that occasion in their *Stockings for a Queen* Milton and Anna Grass suggest that when the Queen 'was handed Lee's pair of coarse woollen stockings, she may have had a feeling of revulsion against the stockings and transferred that feeling to the unfortunate maker of the machine himself. Only silk stockings befitted her royal dignity and position; she, the Queen, no longer wore coarse woollen stockings'.

In order to make finer hose he would have to introduce twenty needles to the inch instead of the eight the machine had originally, but such a modification would take time to perfect. He had to pay his way in the interim and the only means by which he could do this was to sell his knitted goods. Fate was against him since only Freemen of the City could trade within its

Knitting machine c.1770

A hand-operated machine similar to the original stocking frame invented by William Lee in 1589.

walls, and a person could not become a Freeman unless he belonged to the guild for the craft concerned.

All this would have represented a severe drain on his resources, so to ease his financial situation he applied for rooms in Bridewell, a sort of hospital cum poorhouse, whose authorities granted rooms to those who could teach a trade to orphaned children and poor people.

Although some things went well for him, with his invention now capable of knitting silk, his sponsor Lord Hunsdon died and so did the Queen. This ill-fortune disillusioned him and William Lee determined to leave England.

William Lee goes to France
Two Frenchmen, Salomon and Pierre de Caux, had been impressed by what they had heard about William Lee and his recently invented stocking frame and invited him to come to France. William Lee, for his part, may have been attracted by King Henri IV's liberalism and encouragement of free enterprise. In 1608 he took four knitting frames, together with some of his workers, to the dock and saw them loaded on a boat bound for Rouen.

A few years previously a riot had occurred in Paris when hand workers were pushed to action against the machinery. William Lee became worried in case handknitters might take the same stance, in fear that his machines would make them all redundant. These factors seem to have contributed to his decision to return to England. Having sent a gift of some stockings to the Queen of France some time earlier, he made a final appeal to her for help, but this was denied. It appears that before he could make arrangements to return to England, William Lee died of frustration and in poverty in Paris in 1610.

Framework Knitters Established
James Lee had travelled to Paris to visit his brother, but when he arrived found he had died. He decided to implement the plan of bringing back to England the machines and workers, taking all but two of the frame knitters with him. Back in Old Street Square in London James Lee established what was to become the British hosiery industry. James Lee had the ability to carry on with his brother's work, for William Felkin wrote 'there is little doubt (that James Lee) was practically instructed during putting the frame together and in its use. He seems to have been his brother's best workman in it'. By the time he died, in 1657, framework knitting had become well established, not only in London but in other parts of the country as well.

Over the first two centuries from the invention of the knitting machine, this cloud on the horizon of handknitting became darker, and the craft was in danger of being totally eclipsed. The machine knitwear industry gained force, and machine-made garments gradually became cheap and available for the masses. Handknitting as a livelihood was no longer viable. Jobs were created by the new factories of the Industrial Revolution, which attracted people away from handknitting as they brought them higher incomes.

CHAPTER 5
Co-existence And Survival

The number of knitting frames increased greatly in the second half of the seventeenth century. In the early days the framework knitters and the handknitters were able to exist, if somewhat uneasily, side by side. Yet the decline of handknitting was now inevitable and this decline was as noticeable in the great handknitting centres of continental Europe as in England. The initial change was that handknitting as an economic activity was gradually pushed out of the towns to the rural areas, and more specifically to fairly remote parts of the country, such as the Yorkshire Dales and smaller fishing ports.

Handknitting as a craft had reached artistic heights with the Master Knitters' work, but one of the oldest arguments against craftsmanship is that it is not economically viable.

As far as handknitted goods for mass consumption were concerned, it was soon evident that the emerging middle classes were quite happy to pay less for a machine-made substitute rather than high prices for the finely produced quality hand-made goods. At the same time, handknitters were dropping their charges, in an attempt to hold on to their share in the market, to such a pitiful level that it was obvious that they would be better off in some more lucrative employment.

Knitting and its Social Aspects
Handknitting amongst the masses has always had a strong social aspect to it. Competent knitters have been able to talk at the same time as they knitted, even when making the most complex of items, and even average knitters can generally carry on a conversation without dropping too many stitches over simple work. In the Britain of the 1950s it was suggested that the advent of television would see the death of handknitting as a hobby, some claiming that just as people had difficulty in reading whilst knitting, so watching television, a more enthralling pastime, would cause people to lay down their needles. However this was simply not the case because the competent knitter rarely has more than to glance at the work in progress, and can knit most things, except the most complicated, by feel and intuition, and can check what is being done and the progress made without interfering with viewing too much.

Martha Dinsdale, Wensleydale.

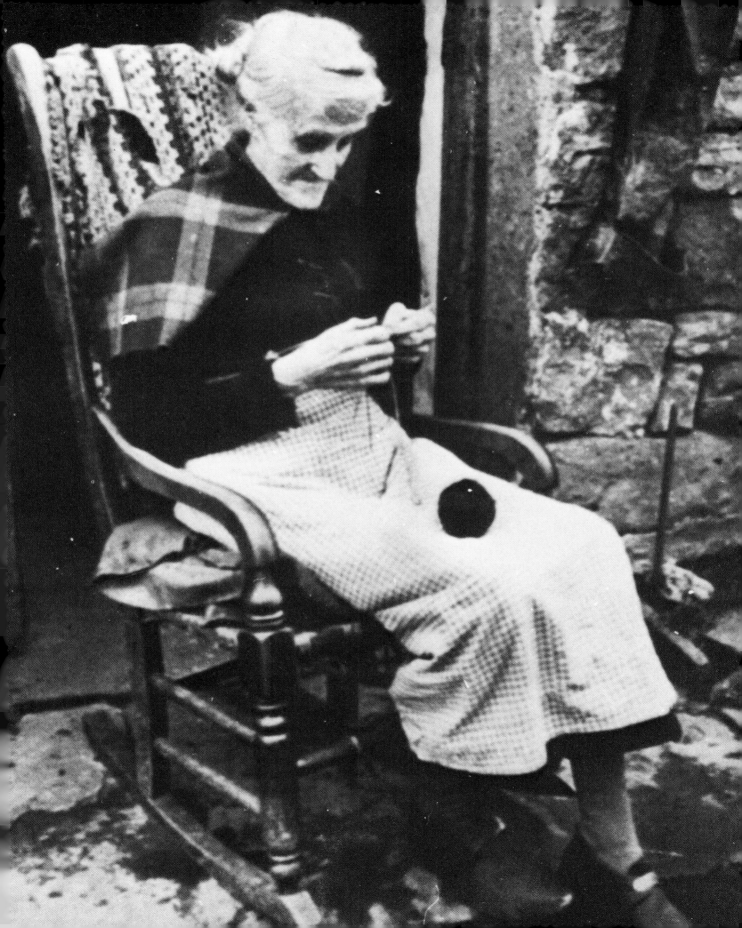

Knitting Sittings and The Dales

Marie Hartley and Joan Ingilby write in their *The Old Handknitters of the Dales:* 'In Dentdale and the Westmoreland Dales most of the womenfolk and children ... contributed their share towards the families' incomes by carding, spinning and knitting ... In the north-west Yorkshire Dales a similar self-contained life prevailed ...'.

The classic description of the social aspect of knitting in small communities comes from William Howitt who, when writing in 1844 about a visit to the Yorkshire Dales, describes the local custom of knitting sittings. He states that wherever he went in the area he always found people knitting, and the knitters would include men and boys as well as women and girls. People would be found sitting on doorsteps knitting, plying their needles as they walked along, or knitting as they travelled in wagons – and not just the passengers knitted but the driver as well. It appears that William Howitt and other visitors to the Dales at that time were surprised to find that the menfolk knitted. William Howitt also describes the schools set up specifically to teach knitting, where children would often sing songs in time with the knitting of rows.

Another writer, Adam Sedgwick, provides a colourful description of the knitting sittings which helps to place the craft nicely in its social context. In a Dale village the neighbours, whether relations or friends, would select a house, usually in rotation, in which to do their knitting for the night. This approach was economical in both light and fuel during the cold, dark winter evenings, and provided a venue for a social get together into the bargain. As darkness fell, and after the evening meal had been finished, neighbours would troop along to the chosen house. The favoured or elder members would have the best seats, the younger ones and any non-knitters (although they would be few) might huddle on the floor on sacks. Members of the group would thus pass the night chatting or recounting tales. In this way legends would be passed on from generation to generation and folklore was created.

The more experienced of the Dales knitters developed a form of hypnotic swaying and rocking in time with their knitting, which was called swaving. The rhythm was supposed to add to the speed at which they could knit. The dull light of a peat fire would only be poked into brightness to allow someone to correct a mistake or knit a complex stitch. The swaving knitting group were said to have appeared as 'weird wizards' in the flickering firelight.

Hustings and Markets

There are many stories concerning knitting in the Dales and they cover a range of topics from politics to murder, adventure and even tax collection. In the eighteenth century when Henry Brougham was standing for election to Parliament he held one of his hustings at Ravenstonedale in Westmorland about 1820. The majority of the audience that he faced were knitting, a sight which so impressed him that he suggested that an appropriate name for the place would be 'Knittingdale!'.

The nearby village of Dent, in Yorkshire, was also immortalised for its knitters. The Lake Poet Robert Southey, in his miscellany *The Doctor* which covers the period from 1834 to 1847, wrote about 'er terrible knitters e' Dent'. In dialect this was paying tribute to the 'great', rather than terrible, knitters of Dent.

The knitters of the Dales produced a variety of garments including jackets

A Borders woollen town in the Industrial Revolution.

and night caps, and that then evergreen of the knitter, the stocking. The caps were particularly interesting in that the knitting to make them was produced a metre in length and then folded to double thickness, much in the style of the Swedish caps of the time. Finished items were taken to the markets. Buyers would go to these markets and collect the produce of a number of knitters for sale elsewhere. A story concerns the old lady, Slinger from Cotterdale, who sold her goods at the market in Hawes. She had to walk three miles to get there from her home. Her visits became a chore to her, but were necessary since she had to do the family's buying and selling there. So as not to waste 'walking time' she knitted throughout her journey. She was able to produce a pair of men's socks during the round trip!

Earnings and Income

Bearing in mind that knitting would not have been the only source of income in the Dales, it must have been a fairly well rewarded one. It is recorded that many of these Dale knitters had incomes high enough to warrant them paying taxes. Nonetheless, the hard-knuckled Dalesmen were notoriously slow at paying up. So the tax collectors, never popular anyway, had to make several visits to extract their dues and were usually met with abuse in the process.

Knitting in the Dales.

Boot Hose

At various times throughout the ages there has been much money to be made from knitting for the troops. The Dales knitters probably provide the first example of this. During the period of the Seven Year War from 1756 to 1763 it was the knitters of Dent who provided many of the specialist stockings worn by the British Army. The best example were the carefully made and perfectly knitted boot hose. Although basically in stocking stitch, these stockings had to be turned at the heel and shaped so that they would fit snuggly into the cavalryman's riding boots. They were folded at the top, to show the only patterned part of them, the horizontally striped top.

Great skill was required to make these boot hose, and those with the necessary skills could gain great financial rewards. The Dentdale knitters had the skill, and so reaped the rewards. They were paid two guineas (£2.10p) per pair, and considerable savings could be amassed.

Sheaths

Perhaps the most touching stories to do with knitting in the Dales do not stem from the knitting itself but rather from an implement used to help in the knitting, the so-called knitting sheath or knitting stick. European knitters had for some time tried to devise ways of making the craft easier and less tiring for the knitter. In knitting, one knitting needle (or knitting pin or knitting prick, words often used in Yorkshire), the one held in the right hand by the right-handed knitter, remains more or less stationary throughout the knitting process, while the other needle is used to do the looping. As the fabric is produced the weight of the work builds up on the left-hand needle, and the larger the item being knitted the more the muscle power required to support the growing work. Various ways were devised to provide this support. The crudest was to gather a bunch of feathers or stems of corn, tightly bind these together and stuff them into a belt. Cloth would also be wound tightly for the same purpose. The stationary needle would be pushed into the feathers or stems and so supported. The Scots developed a form of leather pouch filled with horse or other animal hair, which was then sewn onto a leather belt. The pouch had holes punched in it and the stationary needle would be pushed into one of these to provide support.

The most usual form of support was the knitting stick or sheath. Basically, this was a piece of wood, some 20cm long and 2cm square, into the end of which a hole would be bored or burnt. This knitting stick was then tucked into a belt or tied around the waist with tape, although sometimes it would have a notch cut into the side to enable it to be clipped onto a belt. Once equipped with a knitting stick, the knitter would push the stationary needle into the hole in its end and so support it. In the Dales knitting sticks would frequently be carved in the shape of the wing of a bird, the so called goose wing, type which was very popular, for such a shape would fit more comfortably onto the contours of the knitters' body.

A few examples of knitting sticks found in mainland Europe were made in deer horn or even glass and ceramics rather than wood. However, in England, Scotland and Wales they were invariably made of wood. They came to be love tokens, in much the same way as the Welsh love spoons. They may have been carved by a father for his daughter or by a husband for his wife, and in such cases they could be very elaborate. The material used to make them would be selected with care, sometimes having a sentimental value – for example, wood taken from broken furniture or the beam of a former home, from a tree under which a couple had courted or, in a coastal area, from an old boat.

Unfortunately, these knitting sticks, like handknitting itself, were overtaken by mechanisation and factory-turned sheaths were being sold in shops by the nineteenth century. Today, few knitters realise the benefits to be derived from using a knitting stick and so they have fallen from use.

Knitting in Other Parts of Rural Britain
So far, attention has been concentrated on the survival of the craft in the Dales. However, pockets of handknitters were to be found in rural areas all over Britain in the eighteenth and nineteenth-centuries, all of them playing their part in keeping the craft alive. Knitters in rural areas were countering the constant attack from machine-knitted products, until the craft was able to take on the status of a hobby by the middle of the nineteenth century.

It is significant that these clusters of knitters were, in general, initially centred upon areas where sheep were raised, although later the knitters in these areas got their wool from further afield. So, Dorset, Norfolk and Yorkshire in England, and much of Scotland and Wales, had the 'right ingredients' for the continuance of the craft. The Dorset knitters included shepherds tending their flocks and drovers taking their cattle to market. One should not underestimate the extent to which knitting was still undertaken in these communities; it is not surprising to find that a mother knitted while minding her baby, however it is somewhat more unexpected to find that men knitted while drinking at the local alehouse.

Thus, for some two centuries after William Lee had invented his knitting machine, his 'engine' existed side-by-side with the handknitters. Yet this is not strictly true, for the machine knitter had by then become an urban phenomenon, whereas the handknitter was very much a rural one. The knitters tended to use yarn made on a domestic basis, but as the face of knitting was changing, the method of obtaining yarn was changing too.

CHAPTER 6
Countries Apart:
Mr Baldwin in England;
Mr Paton in Scotland

By the close of the eighteenth century handknitting in Great Britain, as in continental Europe, was heading for extinction. Knitting machines were increasingly taking over, aided by further technical developments and improvements that continued to take place in the course of the Industrial Revolution.

Hargreaves' Spinning Jenny (reconstruction).

Crompton's Spinning Mule (reconstruction).

In 1758 Jedediah Strutt made several alterations to the original machine. In 1847 Matthew Townsend invented a latch needle which was similar to that used on today's domestic knitting machines. William Cotton of the United States developed a power-driven knitting machine in 1864. Machines had to be power driven, and for power-driven machines to be competitive they had to be grouped together in factories. By the middle of the nineteenth century the hosiery and knitwear industry as known today had arrived.

Man had known how to spin yarn for well over five thousand years, using the same primitive technique for most of that time. The initial method of twirling a distaff was replaced by a foot-operated spinning wheel which left both hands free for the manipulation of the fibres. Leonardo da Vinci had produced a drawing of just such a piece of equipment. Between 1764 and 1767 the Spinning Jenny was invented by James Hargreaves, and between 1769 and 1775 Richard Arkwright obtained patents for a combined spinner and roller machine. Between 1774 and 1779 a number of the techniques used in the spinning of yarn were brought together by Samuel Crompton to create the Spinning Mule. These developments emerged for cotton mainly, but were soon adapted to wool.

These inventions constituted one of the factors which led to the revolution in textile production, for it also required an entrepreneurial spirit to exploit the potential. Two people with a flair for commerce and enterprise were a Mr James Baldwin (1746 to 1811) of Halifax in England and a Mr John Paton (1768 to 1848) of Alloa in Scotland, and they did precisely this. Although they did not meet they, and the firms that they established, had many similarities. By the second and third generations of the two families, and before the companies' amalgamation in 1920, there was a long period of intense rivalry.

In their early days, these enterprises mainly produced hosiery yarn for use by machine knitters, but following the revival of handknitting in the form of a leisure pursuit mainly carried out by women, the emphasis of their production from the mid-nineteenth century was increasingly placed on yarns for the home knitter. This proved to be very profitable to the companies, and their product range did much to encourage the growth of handknitting as a fashionable pastime. In time both the Baldwin Beehive and the Paton Rose became synonymous with fashion and quality.

The early generations of the respective families might be surprised to see where the two businesses are now; but they recognised the need for change and growth and maintenance of quality and thrift, which were their watchwords. Today Patons & Baldwins Limited leads in fashion and the innovation of yarns, as well as maintaining the quality of their products.

James Baldwin

James Baldwin was born in Halifax in 1746 and established a wool washing and cloth fulling business there in 1785. This business was situated at Malt Shovel Yard, Northgate, Halifax. He bought in sheep skins from local farmers and these were washed and fulled for resale. Shortly afterwards, he moved his business to Waterside, Halifax, and extended the processing to include carding and both woollen and worsted spinning. James Baldwin was one of the Industrial Revolution's entrepreneurs. He was a strong patriarchal figure, being referred to as 'Father' by all members of the family. When the business expanded he took one of his sons, John, into the firm, and from then on it was styled as J & J Baldwin. Shortly after 'Brother John' entered the business, 'Brother Christopher' also joined and, although there were several comings and goings in the early years, the family involvement remained consistently strong.

'Father' and his family had to live carefully in the early days in order to be able to plough back most of the profits from their labours into the business. Nevertheless, they appear to have lived comfortably. By the third generation, the family had moved into the upper classes.

In this period, the early Industrial Revolution, most businesses kept only one source of accounting records, generally a family ledger which could be used intermittently as a diary. Pieces of family information such as births and deaths, family transactions concerning the purchase of major household wares and recipes and cures for sickness, might be recorded, as in the case of J & J Baldwin's books. Such entries reinforced the fact that the business and life of the owner and his family were much intertwined. There are records of some of the information from the ledger for J & J Baldwin covering the period between 21st September 1804 to 11th August 1809.

The earliest entries appear to have been made by James Baldwin himself and one can imagine him poring over his books late at night, catching up on the paperwork by the light of an oil lamp. Of course the ink eventually became faded and discoloured.

The Early Baldwin Home

James Baldwin's house, his water driven mill, and the warehouses were on the same site. This home in the West Riding of Yorkshire would have been stone-built and two, or perhaps three, storeys high, with some of the workshops likely to have been built attached to the house. Records of the family's private property were included in these early books and provide a valuable insight into the family's interests and life style.

Soon after establishing the business a comfortable existence is indicated for the Baldwin family. The parlour, or sitting room, was furnished with a splendid mahogany table with matching chairs, and there were carpets on the floor and Italian landscapes on the walls. James Baldwin possessed silver cutlery and stocked a cellar.

The inventory of his kitchen cum living room gives ample additional evidence of his success, for there were chandeliers and an extensive assortment of cooking utensils. Upstairs there was enough space for a guest room, and all the bedrooms were comfortably appointed. Solid furniture, as was the fashion of the day, and elegant curtains and bed hangings were listed in the books. There was no skimping on the house, and it is recorded that in the 1800s one of the bedrooms had been refurbished at a cost of over £70.

Perhaps most impressive of all was the cellar. Here there was a small brew-house with barrels of fermenting ale, and a supply of sherry and wines. In the garden would be found the toilet facilities for both the family and the firm (this was referred to as the 'necessary house') and, nearby, the kennels, animals, being both pets and guard-dogs.

The Early Mill
Often nicknames were given to important pieces of equipment. A carding machine bought for £120 was known as the 'old engine' and when a replacement was found, for £300, this was called the 'new engine'. Stocks of card clothing, the large sheets of metal pins to wind round the rollers on the machines, were maintained. Slubbing frames which drew out the carded yarn and wound it on caps, were referred to as the old and the new jack, and the old and the new billy, as additional ones were acquired. The machine for teasing the wool was called a devil. By 1820 the firm had seven spinning jennies, two of which were large for the time, having forty-eight spindles. There was also a roving frame, two spinning frames with seventy-two spindles, and one with eighty-four. One of Crompton's spinning mules is also mentioned, which would probably have been worked by hand rather than by water power, as was much of the machinery.

Side-by-side with this then modern equipment the firm used outworkers, and a stock of hand combs for their use is listed, as were four hand spinning wheels, together with stools for the people who worked them.

To remove the oil from greasy skins and to clean yarns there was a wash house equipped with a scouring pan, tubs and a wringer. A charcoal-burning stove heated water and bellows fanned the fire. Stocks of soap and oils were kept, soap being bought in from Leeds and Liverpool, and whale oil from Hull.

The Finished Yarn
Woollen and worsted yarns of many types and shades were produced by J & J Baldwin and it seems that the firm was continually experimenting with new ideas for different products. Early in the manufacturing process, the wool might be enclosed in a dyeing net, a sort of bag, before being dipped in the dyeing kettle. Dyes at that time still came from natural sources, such as the lichen used to produce purple and voilet, the African red barwood and red

cudbear for reds and log-wood for black. Often the materials for dyeing came from overseas and were bought already shredded. Although Baldwins built a new dye house in 1807, they also sent out wool and yarn to be dyed by other firms.

As well as the black and white yarns, there were the blues, both light and dark, yellow, orange and scarlet as well as red, green, pink and russets. There were drabs and mottles. Other shades had more descriptive names such as sheep grey, clouded blue, milk and water and mulberry. Some of these pioneer colours bore numbers still in use today: such as 51 white, 52 black, 53 white/black mixture, and 55 scarlet.

Lighting in the factory was by oil lamps, but rushlights and candles were also mentioned. Always ready to take up new trends, the company had gas piped to the mill in 1826 for the princely sum of £50, only four years after it had been introduced in Halifax.

Workers were rarely allocated to one task, and would be moved around to operate various types of machinery as necessary. The firm employed its own handyman to maintain the machinery and make repairs. He would also produce small items in wood or metal if required.

James Baldwin, Traveller and Salesman

The production of goods must be complemented by sales, and as well as being an entrepreneur producing yarns, James Baldwin was also a salesman who got out and about – in those days on horseback – and he kept his spurs and crop in the kitchen, where there was also a map of England. Journeys of any significance, say, over one hundred miles, might mean a long period on the road and a great deal of preparation would have been involved prior to his departure, collecting samples of goods and stock.

James Baldwin's journeys would take him all over the North of England and over the border to Scotland, for in the earliest days the firm that was to become J & J Baldwin's greatest rival and ultimate partner had yet to be established. A typical journey for him in the early 1800s was from Halifax, up the west of Lancashire towards Preston, through Lancaster and Workington into Scotland; then on to Dumfries, Paisley and Glasgow. He would then travel across to Edinburgh, down the east coast to Morpeth and through Northumberland into Newcastle, continuing on to Durham and back into Yorkshire through York, and finally home to Halifax. Such a journey might take six weeks. James Baldwin made three such journeys in 1804, one in the depths of winter. The winter journey would have been particularly hazardous, with poor tracks turned into quagmires by rain, and with icy conditions or deep snow elsewhere.

Firms producing different goods frequently acted on behalf of each other during such journeys or traded in the lines of other manufacturers as a side line. The early records kept by the Baldwin family show that footwear, stockings and cloth were also sold at times. Jersey yarns and petticoat wool yarns were always in demand. The range of yarns produced ran from fine lambswool through to thick rug worsted, the latter usually cut into short lengths and pegged into a hessian backing to make a fine rug. This tradition of the sale of rug yarn has come down today in the form of Turkey rug wool for latch-hooking by hand.

James Baldwin would also act as a debt collector, picking up money for the sales he made or from customers who had bought goods from the firm earlier. Records of these transactions, and indeed of his travels themselves, were kept in the so-called travelling books. These also provided a full account of his own purchases and expenses on the journeys. Human error is also shown by periodic complaints, and adjustment of sums concerning the return of soiled yarn, shortages on delivery, even undercharging and miscasting, were all faithfully recorded. There is even evidence of debts which were simply never cleared.

The First Twenty Five Years

James Baldwin died in 1811, having lived some sixty-five years, and the firm he had founded had been running for the last twenty-five of these. During these years he had laid down a firm foundation for the business. His son, 'Brother John' whom he had taken into the business, could build upon what 'Father' had created. James Baldwin left £2,957 when he died – a considerable sum in those times – and this was divided equally between the children. Thus, with his own share which he had already built up in J & J Baldwin and the legacy from his father, the ownership passed in prosperity to the second generation in the shape of 'Brother John'. As will be seen in Chapter 8, he husbanded his inheritance well, adding constructively to the plans laid down by his father. He also led an active social life in which he made solid contributions to his local community.

John Paton

In 1813 in Scotland, some twenty-eight years after James Baldwin had founded his firm, John Paton founded his. Throughout the nineteenth century the two firms became more similar in their product lines and areas of activity – and also in their participation in their respective communities. They were also to become competitors.

It appears that James Paton and his brother Andrew had moved to Alloa from the Muckhart district in the eighteenth century. Andrew set up a dyeing business and James lived in Kilncraig's House, which was on the site of a lime kiln. Hence the name of the Patons factory that was eventually built, and still stands, on this site – Kilncraigs Mill. Nothing is known about what James did for a living but a son John was born in 1768. The boy is likely to have been much influenced by his visits to his Uncle Andrew's dyeing works. It can be imagined that John, as a small boy, would see the drab yarn being dipped into the vats to emerge magically different, all colours of the rainbow. Perhaps encouraged by Andrew, he determined to open his own business. The dilemma of family competition probably arose, and this may have led him to go into the production of yarn itself. Although he was in business for himself in about 1811, it was not until 1813 or 1814 that he took on a two-storey building with basement in the old part of Alloa and there he began in a modest way to become a spinner.

He acquired spinning machinery from England and soon found that dyeing his own yarn would be more profitable; overcoming any qualms he may have previously had about family competition, he installed dyeing equipment. Hand spinning was well established in Scotland at the time but there was little experience of machine spinning. He had to import skilled labour from England to teach the local people. There is no record to suggest how he obtained the necessary capital, or the sources from where it might have been raised. Yet it is obvious that the business was successful. As with the growth of the Baldwin firm, a frugal background and the ability to plough back profits in the crucial early stages of development of the firm, meant that John Paton met with great success. Within a short time the enterprise was expanding and new lands and buildings had to be acquired.

Little is known of John Paton's private life, or even the precise nature of the role he played in the growth of his business. It appears that on his father's death he came into possession of Kilncraig's House, and that this was eventually demolished to make way for a factory extension. Married and with a number of children, his religious background would have encouraged a modest life, certainly more austere than that of the Baldwins. The typical townhouse of the time would have been a two-storey building of grey Scottish stone. He would have bought good, serviceable furniture, and there would certainly have been no cellar or brew-house, for the Patons family were temperate.

The Paton's Mill
Although John Paton had introduced the spinning equipment from England into his mill, his business was a blend of the factory system, based on mechanisation and motive power, and the hand labour of workers in their own cottages. There, the raw wool was initially teased out by hand and was spun on domestic spinning machines. When the first example of Hargreaves' Spinning Jenny was brought to Alloa, and also Crompton's Mule, there were great gatherings not only of the firm's workers but also of the townspeople, and even those living in surrounding areas, to see these marvellous engines. This would have been a special event, and the groups of onlookers can be imagined standing in the streets, congregating around the mill gates and in the mill yard, watching, first silent in awe and then with gasps of amazement, as this totally new, shining equipment was brought slowly along the bumpy streets on carts.

The first thirty-five years saw prosperity and the expansion of John Paton's firm. It is not known whether he engaged in the business of selling his products, or travelling the country as his English counterpart did, or whether his products were sold to merchants who did the selling for him. Nonetheless, he established a successful enterprise and eventually his youngest son Alexander joined him in the firm which was then styled as John Paton & Son. John's two elder sons, James and David, had gone their own way and set up a tweed manufacturing business based in Tillicoultry, the firm of J & D Paton and Company trading under that name until the early 1980s. John Paton died on 12th June 1848, leaving behind him a successful firm renowned for its quality yarns, one which was on course for steady growth in the years to come.

The Separate firms of Baldwins and Patons Firmly Established
At the times that both James Baldwin and John Paton died, they left family firms based securely on good returns, expanding, and similar in many ways. Their sense of propriety went further than their sound business ethics. The founders were friends with many of their workers, as happens in so many family firms. This continued down the generations as can be seen in the welfare provisions made for workers by the growing enterprises. Both families also had a keen sense of community responsibility, and many of their members became involved with aspects of the local society and local government.

However on a wider scale, and seen today as their greatest contribution, were their roles in the continuation of knitting as a craft. A debt is owed to them for their part in the resurgence of the craft of knitting as a leisure pursuit at about the time Victoria came to the throne. Both firms provided a strong impulse for the development of the craft along the lines of a hobby, and eventually into the fashion business it is today. First they produced the quality yarns the handknitters wanted for their garments, and later they (independently of each other) introduced the idea that it was the responsibility of the handknitting yarn spinner to produce effective and simple instructions from which the knitter could make garments for the family and articles for the home. It is this concept which has turned out to be one of the corner stones of the knitting-yarn industry today.

CHAPTER 7
The Craft Becomes A Hobby

Queen Victoria reigned for nearly sixty-four years from 1837 until 1901 – the longest reign of any British monarch. This was a period of national prosperity and confidence at home and abroad. The Industrial Revolution developed apace and the British Empire expanded to the four corners of the globe. What have become known as Victorian values – propriety, the work ethic, sobriety and frugality – have become recognised as the hallmarks of the age.

The Victorian era was a period during which the struggle over handknitting's survival as a craft turned the corner. Handknitting became a respected hobby, initially for gentlewomen, and then gradually for the masses.

Written Knitting Instructions
Up to the golden age of the Master Knitters, knitters had kept the instructions in their head. Experience told them how many stitches to cast on, and how many rows to knit for a given length of fabric. If the knitter knew who the garment was intended for, fittings could be made. For complicated stitch patterns employing many different colours, charts would be drawn up.

Nevertheless, people gradually became familiar with certain codes, or shorthand, which could be used to designate more complicated instructions. In 1588 – the year before William Lee invented the knitting machine – Dr Timothy Bright invented a code which he dedicated to Queen Elizabeth I. In 1837 Isaac Pitman published his method for taking shorthand.

By the 1800s it was a natural step to apply a known concept to record knitting instructions in an abbreviated form. Exactly when the more or less standard form of abbreviations used in knitting patterns – on the lines of K, P, inc, sl, yrn – came into general usage is not certain. Some form of shorthand for knitting instructions was being printed in books by 1840, in *The Lady's Assistant* by Mrs Jane Gaugain. These codes are easy to follow and present no insurmountable problems for those who are not particularly good readers. Illiteracy was still widespread, but the abbreviated form of knitting instructions could be understood with minimal education. Women's magazines started to include knitting patterns, although relatively few until late in the nineteenth century. These may have stimulated a wider interest in knitting as a hobby, or it may have been a growing interest in knitting that promoted the publication of knitting 'recipes'.

At this time, crochet had no major role as either an industry or a pastime, although it had a history as long as that of knitting. It was often referred to as "Shepherds knitting".

THE
LADY'S ASSISTANT
FOR
Executing Useful and Fancy Designs
IN
KNITTING, NETTING, AND CROCHET WORK.

ILLUSTRATED BY FIFTEEN ENGRAVINGS, SHOWING VARIOUS STITCHES IN THE ART OF NETTING.

BY MRS GAUGAIN.

SECOND EDITION.

PUBLISHED BY I. J. GAUGAIN,
FOREIGN AND BRITISH DEPOT OF BERLIN PATTERNS AND MATERIALS FOR LADIES' FANCY WORKS,
63, GEORGE STREET, EDINBURGH;
AND ACKERMANN & CO. LONDON.
1840.
Price Five Shillings and Sixpence, Handsomely Bound in Cloth.

Front cover of "The Lady's Assistant" by Mrs Gaugain.

LIST OF PATRONESSES AND SUBSCRIBERS, ALPHABETICALLY ARRANGED.

Her Majesty the QUEEN DOWAGER.
Her Royal Highness the Duchess of GLOUCESTER.
Her Royal Highness the Duchess of CAMBRIDGE.
Her Royal Highness the Princess AUGUSTA CAROLINA.

Argyle, Her Grace the Duchess of	Arbuthnott, Lady Jane	Dundas, Lady, of Beechwood
Atholl, H. G. the Duchess of	Balfour, Lady E.	Dalrymple, Lady Ferguson
Buccleuch, H. G. the Duchess of	Barrington, Rt. Hon. Lady Caroline	Elibank, Right Hon. Lady
Gordon, H. G. the Duchess of	Blantyre, Right Hon. Lady	Gifford, Right Hon. Lady
Leeds, H. G. the Duchess of	Campbell, Lady, of Succoth	Glenlyon, Rt. Hon. Dow. Lady
Northumberland, H. G. Duchess of	Campbell, Lady Hume	Gomm, Lady
Roxburgh, H. G. the Duchess of	Carnegie, Lady, of Southesk	Cumming Gordon, Lady
Douro, M. N. the Marchioness of	Carnegie, Lady Jane	Greenock, Right Hon. Lady
Lothian, M. N. the Marchioness of	Cathcart, Rt. Hon. Lady Mary	Hay, Right Hon. Lady Mary
Tweeddale, M. N. Marchioness of	Cathcart, Rt. Hon. Lady Augusta	Hope, Rt. Hon. Lady Frances
Dalhousie, Rt. Hon. Countess of	Clinton, R. H. Lady, Devonshire	Howick, Right Hon. Lady
Gray, Right Hon. the Countess of	Colville, Lady	Keith, Lady, Ravelstone
Hopetoun, Rt. Hon. Countess of	Dalrymple, Lady Adamina	Kerr, Right Hon. Lady Robert
Morton, Rt. Hon. the Countess of	Douglas, Lady Christian	Kinloch, Lady Gilmerton
Strathmore, Rt. Hon. Countess of	Douglas, Lady W. Grangemuir	Lockhart, Lady Norman
Wemyss, Rt. Hon. the Countess of	Drummond, Lady, of Hawthornden	Majoribanks, Lady
Arbuthnott, Rt. Hon. Viscountess	Dundas, Rt. Hon. Lady Mary	M'Kenzie, Lady Muir
Melville, Right Hon. Viscountess	Dundas, Lady Dunira	M'Kenzie, Lady

Part of the list of sponsors, totalling over five hundred, who supported Mrs Gaugain's "The Lady's Assistant".

(Colour)
Rural Britain

A WELSH GROUP under the Old Cross of St. Davids.

Knitting Books
The earliest known knitting book appears to have been printed in Germany. *Die Kunst zu stricken in ihrem ganzen Umfange* (The Art of Knitting in all its Aspects), by Netts and Lehmann, was published in Leipzig in 1800. This was at a time when the Germans were the major innovators in dyeing techniques and when Berlin wool, famous for its colour, was reaching worldwide fame.

The date of the earliest British knitting book is difficult to ascertain. The Misses Watts produced in 1837 *The Ladies' Knitting and Netting Book*; with the book produced by Mrs Gaugain in 1840, perhaps the best known of those from that period. It is interesting to find a certain Mrs Beeton also tried her hand in this field, producing books with knitting 'recipes' in them, although it appears that the designs in these were commissioned or purchased from others.

Many of these books were supported by sponsors. Mrs Gaugain's *The Lady's Assistant* was sponsored by over 500 people, including HM The Queen Dowager, the Duchess of Gloucester and the Princess Augusta Caroline. This work was published in Edinburgh in 1840 and obtainable in I J Gaugain's shop in that city.

The contents of such books provide a good indication of the clothing of the times, with instructions for chemises, vests, petticoats and 'gentlemen's bosom friends', as well as spencers and bonnets. Although Mrs Gaugain's book, like many of the early books in this field, was produced for the gentlewoman, she eventually published *The People's Knitting Book* – good business for her shop?

Women's Magazines
The earliest forerunner of today's women's magazines may have been *The Ladies' Mercury,* a broadsheet which was brought out in 1693. This consisted of forthright answers to readers' enquiries on love, marriage and fashion. The publication of magazines started to take off in the period from the late eighteenth century to the middle of the nineteenth century, aimed almost exclusively at the middle classes.

Mass circulation had two major obstacles to overcome: the problem of illiteracy, and the fact that paper for printing was not cheap. The nation lacked a means of distributing publications until spending power was available to the masses. Publications of the time were very expensive; some had hand-engraved fashion plates from Paris, sometimes being hand-coloured.

In 1852 Mrs Isabella Beaton introduced *The English Woman's Domestic Magazine* which provided paper patterns for dress-making, instructions for embroidery, and eventually knitting instructions, Credit should be attributed to Mrs Weldon who founded *The Ladies' Journal* in 1879, a magazine which included many features, and was published until 1954, when it was incorporated with another magazine. Mrs Weldon's magazine spawned a great many specialist publications in the needlecraft field, and in turn led to the famous series of Weldon's knitting leaflets. By the end of the nineteenth century the utility journals had become established, limiting themselves to home-making and women's fiction. The contents of these publications would be considered both comfortable and comforting to their readers, disseminating a homely philosophy which lasted until the inter-war years.

The architect of the modern women's magazine can be said to be Winifred 'Biddy' Johnson who edited *Forget Me Not,* published by the Amalgamated Press, and first issued in 1891. It featured home management, and advice on

(Top left and right) **Cover illustrations from Beehive Knitting Booklets**
(bottom left) **Advertisement from 1906** *(bottom right)* **Cover for** *Stitchcraft* **magazine for February 1933**

making clothes for the family. By 1894 its circulation had reached 141,000, larger than all the other comparable publications combined. In 1894 Pearson's *Home Notes* was published; *Home Chat,* which was published by Harmsworth in 1895, soon became the main rival to *Forget Me Not* with a circulation of 185,000. *Home Chat* aimed to provide a weekly publication for women, selling for one penny (½p) while maintaining the quality of similar publications which sold for sixpence (2½p).

Availability of Yarns

A factor in the growth of knitting during the Victorian period was the more widespread and increasing availability of knitting yarns. In earlier days

villagers had spun the yarn for their own requirements. In the sheep farming areas of the country, few cottages would be without a spinning wheel. However, the advent of industrialisation meant that there was an exodus from the rural areas into the towns where employment was more certain. Industry drew in women as well as men, and the hours worked were often long, leaving little or no time for leisure pursuits. It was rare to find a spinning wheel in houses in the now expanding towns, and the womenfolk would not be expected to spin yarn after a day at the factory.

The demand for knitted goods did not slacken, so a market for factory-produced knitting yarns filled the gap, and many small spinners started up. The yarns produced were of varying quality and were often sold by pedlars or travelling salesmen. Shops were developing in towns, along the lines of today's corner shops, which needed a regular supplier of knitting wools, and could not depend upon the small spinner. It was left to the larger, expanding spinners, such as J & J Baldwin and John Paton & Son, to fulfil this need.

Knitting Needles

The main materials used to produce knitting needles today are aluminium, plastic and wood – the former a substitute for older metals such as steel, and

Advertisement from 1896

plastic a substitute for bone or ivory. It appears that the sizing of knitting needles did not become standardised at any particular time. Writers of mid nineteenth century knitting books eventually had to provide some guidance as to the size of needles. By the second series of *My Knitting Book* by Miss Lambert, published in 1847, the author had already devised a *Standard Filière* to enable the knitter ascertain the size of knitting pins for the designs in her book — a forerunner of today's knitting needle gauges. The book states that this had been 'invented' some time ago by Miss Lambert and was now in 'general use', and that, using this, 'the different sizes of knitting . . . needles can now be ascertained with the greatest accuracy'.

The Lady's Knitting Book, written by E.M.C. in 1884, states 'The standard of measurement for the pins is Chamber's Bell gauge', and in the book needles made of ivory are mentioned, as well as bone, wood and steel. However, it is the second edition of *The Hand-Book of Plain and Fancy Knitting,* which was published by Webb and Millington of Leeds, probably in the 1860's, and written by an unnamed author who also wrote *Etiquette of Love, Courtship and Marriage,* that provides a major clue when it states: 'Necessary Implements for Knitting. Needles of various sizes are used. Those referred to in this book are of the Knitting Needle gauge. The Gauge is a circular piece of steel, finished in beautiful style. Various opinions are afloat respecting the standard measure; — some claiming it as their own invention, while others repudiate it altogether. The gauge referred to in these pages has been in use for centuries, and is the standard used in wire manufactories to regulate their size. It may be procured from any Whitesmith or Ironmonger.'

Knitting needles were called knitting pins, knitting wires or knitting pricks, according to region, and would have been made by local craftsmen. When migration to urban areas started there was a need to be able to buy needles in local shops.

Henry Milward provides an example of the establishment of a needle firm which also produced knitting needles. In 1730 he founded a company at Washford Water Mill, on the River Arrow at Redditch in Worcestershire. The firm produced all sorts of needles although it is not recorded when knitting needles were first mass produced; Milward needles are now world famous. The firm has gone through a series of amalgamations over the years and is now incorporated in the Needle Industries Group Ltd, part of Coats Patons PLC.

Abel Morrell, also of Redditch, manufacture Aero knitting pins. Aero's old catalogues show a steel knitting pin from the early 1900s. In 1930 the firm made knitting needles from vulcanite, nickel plated steel and Erencod, a type of plastic. The "Aero" knitting pin, with the grey anodised coat, was first manufactured in 1933 and has remained the firm's top brand since.

Thus, knitting needle producers sprang up during the nineteenth century. The problem was that there was no standardisation in sizing, and this became necessary as different bodies started to publish instructions. When bone pins were used little attention was paid to accurate sizing. During the nineteenth century, the availability of wire to make steel knitting pins led to standardisation. As none of the manufacturers had a wire drawing plant they were dependent on the Black Country wire drawers who worked to the standard wire gauges. Therefore, the British needle sizings from 12 to 5 (·104inch to ·432inch) were exactly the same as the standard wire gauge. Today pins are made from one of two materials. Plastic, currently made from polystyrene, and used to make needles on electronically controlled moulding machines, or grey aluminium, bought in coils of the required diametre, solid for the small sizes and tubular for the heavy gauges. In the 1970s knitting needle sizing moved over to use the metric system.

Woolshops

By the Tudor period some specialisation had occurred in the distribution of goods in towns. Originally it was the haberdasher, and later the draper, who would stock knitting yarns amongst the range of smallwares or clothing they held. By the Victorian period it was the drapery shop which had become well established and stocked knitting wools. Nevertheless, the tally man and the market were still important methods of distribution and the departmental store was on the horizon.

The earliest recorded woolshop was that founded by John Smith in Glasgow in 1796. William Hunter also established wool retailing businesses in Northumberland in the middle of the nineteenth century. Another woolshop was set up more or less by accident in Greenock, Scotland, in 1881. Over forty years before this, John Fleming and James Reid, who were brothers-in-

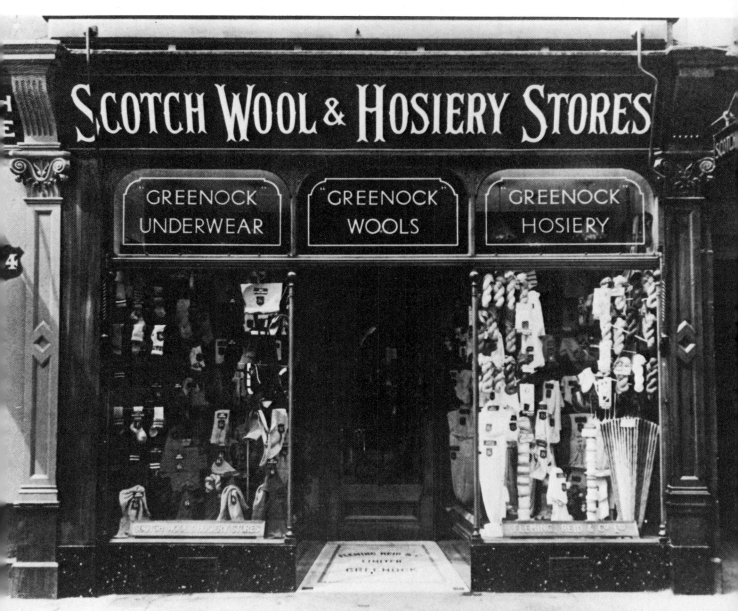

In its heyday, the "Scotch Wool Shop" chain had over three hundred branches.

law, established a spinning mill with a third partner, Robert Neil, who died in 1855. The partnership then became Fleming, Reid and Company. In 1881 a manufacturing customer returned a large amount of tweed wool as it was not the correct shade. A decision was made to twist it to produce a yarn which could sell cheaply to employees for knitting. Friends and relations saw these employees knitting with the yarn and wanted some. The company identified a need and started to produce yarn especially for the handknitter, opening a small shop in Greenock to sell to the public. From this grew the national chain of woolshops, under the style of Scotch Wool & Hosiery Co., which eventually had over three hundred branches.

It was unusual in the Victorian period to find shops which sold only, or even mainly, knitting yarn. It was not until the twentieth century that the independent specialist woolshops as known today really started.

The Spinners Leaflets

As the demand for handknitting yarns grew, some of the enlightened spinners realised that, if they produced instructions for knitters, as well as providing a service it would encourage the knitter to use more of their yarns.

One of the first attempts at this was the production of the *Knitting and Crochet Book* by John Paton, Son and Company of Alloa in 1896. This book, which was priced one shilling (5p), ran to 228 pages and included over one

The "Knitting & Crocheting Book" was produced by John Paton, Son & Co. in 1896. It was priced at one shilling (5p) and contained over one hundred designs for all the family.

62

hundred designs for all the family. Largely because of the success of this, in 1899 the firm produced the *Universal Knitting Book,* which was priced at one penny (½p) and ran through three editions before being combined with Baldwins *Woolcraft,* which was first produced shortly before the amalgamation of the two firms.

By the end of the Victorian era the concept of knitting instructions had arrived and within the first decade of the twentieth century all major spinners were producing these as pamphlets, the forerunners of today's leaflets. The variety of knitting yarns, both in quality and colour, was increasing. There had also been some standardisation in the thicknesses of yarn into the two, three and four plys with which we are familiar today.

Knitting In Schools

A major impetus was given to knitting by the Education Act of 1870. In her *Directions for Knitting Socks and Stockings,* published in 1883 under the direction of The Committee of General Literature and Education appointed by the Society for Promoting Christian Knowledge, Mrs Lewis states 'Knitting is an art which has been practised in England for many centuries, though in the last few generations it has fallen somewhat into disuse. The Education Act of 1870 has endowed it with new life and vigour, which bid fair to strengthen year by year, for now every girl *must* be taught to knit. She is not to be left to pick it up (if she be inclined) anyhow, – to do a few stitches at her granny's knee and then to forget all about it; but knitting is to be part of the education which, in these days, every girl must receive, and she is to be taught so thoroughly that she is to be able to knit socks and stockings as well. There can be no question but that it was a very wise judgement which made knitting compulsory in National Schools.' Mrs Lewis goes on to say that 'knitting gives a certain dexterity of finger most valuable in all future work, and is a great help in educating the eye, – advantages which can scarcely be over-estimated.'

In another of her books, *Wools and How to Use Them,* published a year later, Mrs Lewis says that through the advent of the sewing machine 'a clever worker has a great deal more time at her disposal, which she can employ pleasantly to herself and more profitably to her family by knitting.' She goes on to say that 'Since the Education Act of 1870, the art of knitting has made enormous progress among the working classes. Previous to that time it was almost unknown in England; Scotland and Wales seeming to have a proprietary right in it, and while it was a matter of course that the Scotch Fisherwife and the Welsh Dairymaid should always be knitting, the Englishwoman's fingers were idle, at those times, such as going to market, or taking a journey, when she might have been at work. It will, I fear, be a long time before we see the Englishwoman take out her knitting in the train, or knit as she walks along the road as the Scotch and Welsh have done for years; but we shall, I hope, arrive at that result in time. Knitting is now taught in all Elementary Schools as part of the Education Scheme, there is no option, it is *compulsory* for girls and is recommended for boys.'

If one reads the log books written up by Head Teachers in the late nineteenth century to provide a diary of what was taught, it will be seen that knitting is usually well represented. Today the Knitting Craft Group of the British Hand Knitting Association provides teaching material which it encourages teachers to use when the craft is not compulsory.

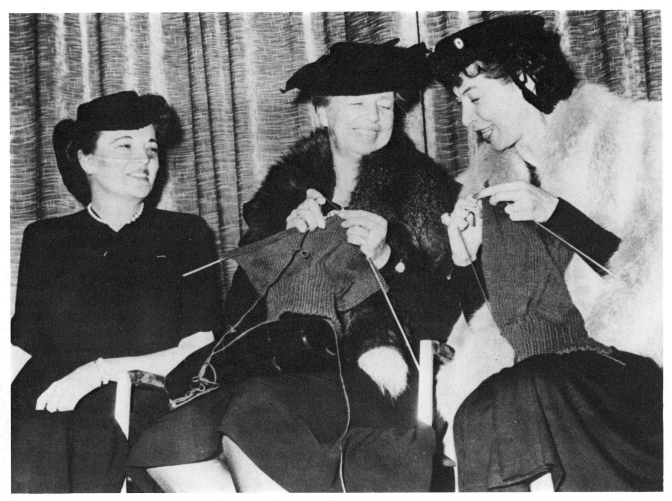

Eleanor Roosevelt *(centre)*.

Knitting for War and Disaster

In Chapter 5 it was seen how boot hose were knitted for the cavalryman. There are many examples of handknittings used by the military. When the craft became a hobby, women's working parties would produce knitted items for the troops.

Perhaps the first royal knitter for the war effort was Queen Victoria. It appears that she must have knitted since childhood. In her journal on the 9th April 1841 she wrote 'Albert read to me out of 'Oberon', whilst I knitted...'* Queen Victoria knitted four scarves to be given to the four most distinguished private soldiers in Colonial regiments serving in the Boer War (1899-1902) — Private Thompson, Canada; Private Duprayer, New South Wales; Private Coutts, New Zealand and Trooper Chadwick, Cape Colony.

On both sides of the Atlantic knitting for the troops was well organised by the time of the First World War. One famous knitter for the war effort in both World Wars was Eleanor Roosevelt, the wife of President Franklin D. Roosevelt of the United States of America. Margaret Bassett wrote 'World War 1 closed out much of Washington's social life and Eleanor turned to the Red Cross and the Naval Hospital. A great knitter, it was natural for her to help

*This quotation is used by the gracious permission of Her Majesty the Queen.

organise the knitting of various articles that the Red Cross fancied would keep the doughboys warm in their trenches'. Mrs Roosevelt was still carrying on the good work in World War 2. Mary Hornady, writing in 1941, said that over one million women from Red Cross Chapters in the United States of America volunteered to knit sweaters for soldiers, continuing 'In New York City, Mrs Eleanor Roosevelt stopped off at the Waldorf-Astoria ballroom to knit a row in the first sweaters of an expected 1,000,000 more to be knitted ... "I hope you do better than we did 20 years ago", Mrs Roosevelt candidly told the women who watched her knit a row. Quite bluntly she recalled that during the last war many garments had to be unravelled and reknitted'.

In Britain King George VI's wife, Queen Elizabeth (now The Queen Mother) used to knit – especially in support of the country's war effort in both the First and Second World Wars, as did her two daughters in the Second. Angus Hall, writing about Princess Elizabeth (now Queen Elizabeth II) said about the early days of the war 'Together with Margaret, her war effort then mainly consisted of knitting woollen socks and mufflers for servicemen abroad – and for Philip in particular'.

In peace time knitting efforts have been directed towards disasters or charities and recently the knitters themselves have been sponsored thus raising funds as well as providing useful warm woollen garments.

The Domestic Knitting Machine

Although domestic knitting machines as known in the second half of the twentieth century were unknown in the nineteenth century, there were the

The Queen Mother and her two daughters.

The Cambridge crew, 1921, displaying a fine array of knitted garments.

so-called sock machines, and the question as to whether these were likely to oust the handknitting of socks and stockings is well answered by Mrs Lewis in her *Directions for Knitting Socks and Stockings,* published in 1883, when she says 'It has sometimes been said of knitting . . . "Why take all that trouble, and spend so much time upon a thing which can be done so much better by machine?" At first sight there appears some force in the argument, but it will not bear looking into. The present high price of the knitting-machine prevents it being widely used, and, unless it becomes much cheaper, it will be unknown in the cottage.' She continues that 'the machine will never supersede hand-knitting. There will still be those who like knitting for its own sake; like to have it to take up at odd times; to whom knitting is a source of pleasure to themselves and profit to their poor neighbours".

The Knitting Mania

By the end of the Victorian period, the scene for knitting as a hobby had been set. At times during this period knitting reached fanatical proportions, and it became the thing for women to knit and be seen knitting. A satirist of the period composed a song called *The Knitting Mania,* which started off:

'They are all knitting, knit, knit, knitting,
They are all knitting at our house at home....'

Everything was knitted — for men, women, children and babies; outer garments, undergarments; items for the home; toys — in short, anything that could be knitted.

The knitting mania showed no sign of abatement during the twentieth century. The Guinness Book of Records, 1962 edition, states world duration record for non-stop knitting was claimed by Felicity Ashton Valerie Cleverton and Patricia Ford who knitted squares for blankets to be used by refugees. They did this outside Bristol University in March 1960. The 1972 edition shows this had been broken by 1971 when Janice Marwick of New Zealand knitted for 90 hours with 5 minute time outs allowed per hour. The same edition says that the most prolific handknitter of all time was Gwen Matthewman of West Yorkshire who in 1970 knitted 615 garments using about 200 kilograms of yarn, the equivalent of the fleece from 57 sheep. The 1984 edition notes that Mrs Matthewman was timed at 111 stitches per minute in 1980.

At the dawn of the twentieth century everything looked favourable for the continuance of the craft — the spinners were producing yarns in a range of qualities and an extensive colour choice. Knitting pins suitable for all kinds of projects were readily available, knitting instructions had taken a firm place in the contents of women's magazines, and the spinners themselves produced their own series of knitting leaflets.

CHAPTER 8
Growth On Both Sides Of The Border

The Victorian transition of handknitting from a cottage industry into a pastime followed by most women was without doubt helped along by John Paton & Son and J & J Baldwin and Partners, who were amongst the leading knitting yarn spinners of the day.

The question as to whether firms such as these created the market, or reacted to supply an existing demand, cannot be answered satisfactorily. For in truth it was not a chicken-and-egg situation; the two developments occurred side by side and served to reinforce each other.

North of the Border
John Paton died in 1849, leaving his son Alexander Paton as the sole owner. He brought into the business his brother-in-law, Alexander Forrester, and a nephew, John Thompson. Three members of the family were now involved, but only one with the Paton name. The two men without the family name changed their names by deed poll to Alexander Forrester-Paton and John Thompson-Paton. They did have Paton blood, but they had descended down the female line. Shortly after, they were made partners of the firm and the company was styled John Paton, Son & Company. On the death of Alexander Paton on 18th September 1860, only just over a decade after his father, the ownership and management of the firm passed to the third generation of Patons.

The Partnership Contracts
Although there is no equivalent to the Baldwin books for the Paton family, and there is little detailed information on the first two generations of the Patons, more evidence comes to light from 1860 onwards with the availability of the contracts of co-partnership until the firm became a limited company in 1906. While Alexander Paton was at the helm, the firm enjoyed a period of consolidation, yet at his death in 1860 the capital required to operate the firm under the new partnership was only £10,000 (though this was a considerable sum of money in those days). Paton's real expansion began from this date. Interest and participation in handknitting as a hobby was taking off, and with a growing market for its products and a well established reputation for quality yarns, it was not long before Scottish yarns in general, and Alloa yarns in particular, achieved worldwide fame and sales.

Alexander Forrester-Paton, the senior partner, was responsible for the overall management of the firm. The contract of co-partnership between Alexander and John Thompson-Paton was to last for fourteen years and each partner was paid a quarterly salary of £75, with any profits to be shared equally between them, but left in the business. The brother of the junior partner, David Thompson, and his brother-in-law, Robert Procter, joined the firm in due course, Procter as the firm's accountant. Eventually, these two men were also made partners and a new contract of co-partnership was drawn up in 1873. This was to run for six years and increased the capital in the firm by over six times the amount necessary in 1860, to £64,000. Price levels were relatively stable in that period, so this indicates that phenomenal growth had taken place.

Alexander Forrester-Paton then went into retirement, the new contract making no provision for his salary, and stipulating that he was to step in only if John Thompson-Paton died before him.

On the death of Alexander Forrester-Paton in 1883, John Thompson-Paton became Chairman. In 1885 the capital of the partnership was increased to £162,000, with interest to be paid on capital and profits to be shared in relation to holdings, but there was no provision for partners' salaries. However, partners could make withdrawals from the firm of up to £2,000 a year from the interest on their capital and their share of profits, and more if all the partners agreed, but capital was to remain intact.

Expansion in the Third Generation

In 1860, the year Alexander Paton died, the factory was burnt down, and this meant largely rebuilding from scratch. In 1837 John Paton had employed 80 people, but after the rebuilding in 1861 the partnership employed around 150

Kilncraigs Mill, Alloa, 1871.

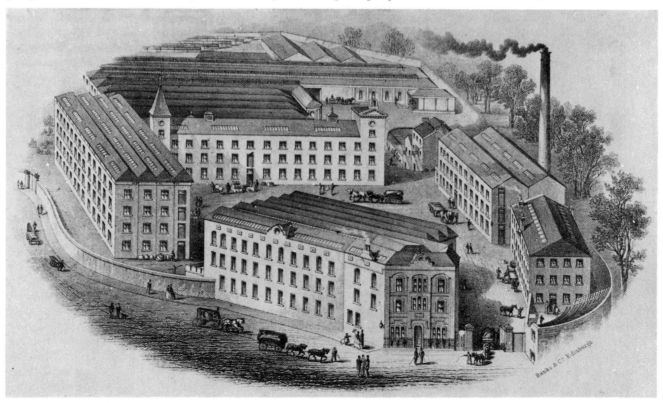

people. The reconstruction of the Kilncraigs factory now included the Burnside Mill and within the next ten years the firm bought the North mill. By 1872 the number of carding machines had grown to thirty and there were 450 employees. The expansion was to meet demand for knitting yarns and tweed and hosiery yarn production carried on side by side. Nevertheless, knitting yarns were significant with the spinning of *wheeling* at the top of the list and the production of *fingering* being added in 1872.

In 1883, the new Chairman, John Thompson-Paton, had his own ideas to propel the firm forward into a new era of dynamic growth. Wool, the staple raw material of the firm, was all important, and although the comparatively small production targets of the early days could be met by local wool suppliers, this was no longer true. By the 1850s the firm was having to look further afield for adequate supplies of good quality wool. This initially meant bidding in the English market, but as time passed Australia proved a vital source in keeping the machines, and users' demands, supplied. Australian wool was bought through middlemen in London and the fleeces tended to be inferior to those that could be purchased on the spot in Australia.

So John Thompson-Paton took the adventurous step of sending the firm's wool buyer, Andrew Cowie, to Australia to buy direct. This was a gamble which paid off handsomely. By the turn of the century the stock of over 900,000 kilograms weight of wool held by the firm (valued then at £135,000) was of the highest quality. Problems regarding storage arose and this necessitated the building of additional wool stores in Alloa.

The Patons Rose
Paton's Alloa yarns grew steadily in popularity. In *The Lady's Knitting-book* by E.M.C., published in 1884, instructions are provided for a slipper in Alloa yarn. Smaller firms, trying to cash in on the popularity of knitting wool and the reputation of Patons, passed off far inferior yarns under the generic name of Alloa. To counter this Patons adopted a trade mark. The mark was what has become the famous Paton's "rose", and the motto 'Virtute Viget' means essentially 'it thrives by its goodness'. It was an apt claim by a firm whose products had indeed become synonymous with consistent quality, witnessed by the fact that by the end of the nineteenth century the firm was producing over 450,000 kilograms weight of yarn a year. On 15th May 1877 the name John Paton, Son & Company, Alloa was registered, with the number 12037 being given by the Registrar of Trade Marks. On 29th April 1885 the "Rose and hand" device received the registration number 44687, and on 24th September 1888 the "White heather and bonnet" device became number 80526.

By now much of the old town of Alloa had been covered by Paton's factory and warehouse buildings. Local smaller firms which had tried to ride to success on the back of Patons were now bought out in order to provide the necessary additional facilities.

The key to the siting of a yarn manufacturing plant is an adequate water supply and by 1875 the water supply in Alloa was simply insufficient. So the firm expanded into neighbouring Clackmannan where water could be drawn from the Black Devon river. Although this was merely a branch factory, it was a major development in its own right. The four-storey mill was equipped with twelve carding machines and forty-two spinning mules. Expansion continued: in 1900 Springfield Mill and its water rights were purchased; in 1903 three storeys were added to the West Mill; in 1904 a new office block was built; in

1905 a new tower tank and sprinkler plant; in 1908 additional boilers installed.

Over this period the Procter side of the family became more involved in the firm. The granddaughter of John Paton married Robert Procter. His two sons Robert and William became trainees in the business and eventually executives. Robert died young in 1897, but William Procter became Chairman of the Private Limited Company formed in 1906, and the first Vice-Chairman of the merged organization in 1924, a position he held for fourteen years.

Sales

In the early days the firm had a policy in Scotland of selling its handknitting products through wholesalers, rather than to retailers, although in England it would supply some of the larger retailers direct. By the time of the merger Patons had a large British sales force and warehouses in London, Manchester and Belfast as well as Alloa. Overseas, warehouses were to be found in Australia and Canada, in addition to agents who sold on behalf of Patons in many other countries.

Knitting Instructions

The firm soon became aware that people knitting as a hobby were unable to take the traditional approach of carrying patterns in their head. In Chapter 7 it

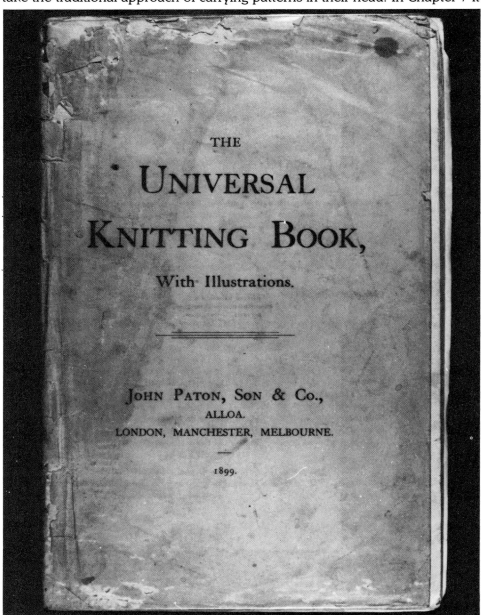

Front cover of "The Universal Knitting Book". This very successful book was priced at one penny (½p) and ran through three editions before eventually being combined with Baldwins' "Woolcraft".

72

"Doing her bit!"

"Paton's" is the Wool for "Comforts"

FOR *Socks* that will *last,* and keep soft and "comfy" all the time, use Paton's Wheelings, Super and Rose qualities. For *Helmets, Mufflers, Mitts,* etc., you will find Paton's Double-Knitting, Fingerings and Petticoat Wools unsurpassed.

(Patterns free on request).

All Paton's Wools are made in Britain by British Workers.

PATON'S Alloa Knitting Wools

FREE BOOK *"How to Knit Soldiers' and Sailors' Comforts,"* post free 1½d. in stamps.

Paton's, Alloa, Scotland, also at 192, Aldersgate Street, London.

Advertisement from 1915

was seen that in 1896 the *Knitting and Crochet Book,* and in 1899 *The Universal Knitting Book,* were produced. The latter proved very popular and was constantly being revised. In addition, in the early 1900s booklets of *'Helps to Knitters'* were issued, which were the forerunners of the knitting leaflets.

The First Twenty Years of the Twentieth Century

Robert Procter, the firm's accountant partner, died on 12th January 1906 and the partnership was then converted into a Private Limited Company with a share capital of £700,000, which had been increased to nearly one million pounds by 1918. John Thompson-Paton became the first Chairman and with him the firm had four directors, all of whom were members of the family. John Thompson-Paton died on 3rd February 1910 having provided a dynamic leadership to the firm for some twenty-seven years, during which the business enjoyed unprecedented growth and prosperity.

Social Responsibilities
Employee Welfare and Community Involvement

The founder John Paton had been raised in a devoutly religious family and the family continued to be conscientious churchgoers. This influenced their feelings towards the local community and their employees. They were involved in community activities and played a major role in the development of Alloa itself. Patons had great influence on the economic and social well-being of the town, in that most families had one or more members employed there and so the prosperity of the town relied heavily on the firm.

Mill managers such as John Cowie, whose son Andrew was the pioneering buyer sent to Australia, John France, whose son Harry also became a mill manager, and Allan Andrews, who was a factory engineer, represent just a few of the dozens of men who formed a loyal and harmonious cadre of managers and who, though not part of the family, helped the expansion and prosperity of the firm. John Cowie was held in such high regard that in December 1929 the Directors of what was now Patons & Baldwins Limited from both Alloa and Halifax attended a dinner to celebrate his fifty years' service. He was presented with a magnificent silver candelabrum suitably inscribed, and Mrs Cowie was given a beautiful diamond brooch. It was said at the time that it was hoped that he would continue 'in harness' for many years to come.

Alexander Paton built a school to provide free elementary education for employees' children and young workers at a time when schooling had to be paid for. When free compulsory education was eventually introduced in 1870, the building was transformed into a works canteen. On the Sabbath the building was used as a Sunday school and for bible classes. Before pension schemes were initiated Patons granted pensions to employees with long service. There were day trips from the mills – the first being recorded in 1860. A special train was hired to take all the employees away to the Clyde or the Firth of Forth or some other beauty spot. On the big day the mill would empty and a procession, led by a band, would troop down to Alloa station to board the train. Armed with picnics the party would embark on what, for many, would be their only holiday.

In 1888 John Thompson-Paton commissioned the building of a town hall which incorporated a library and reading room, and this he presented to the town. Ten years later he provided the funds for a swimming pool and gymnasium. When Parliament designated the Scottish Commission Boards as Town Council, David Thompson was elected as the first Provost. Alexander Forrester-Paton was a Chairman of the Alloa Burgh School Board and built and equipped the High Grade School which he presented as a gift to the Board. Similarly a Model Workshop was set up for instruction in manual skills. Robert Procter took an active interest in Sunday school work and built a hall with a suite of rooms for this purpose which was presented to his church.

From the foundation of the Paton dynasty in 1813, members of the family nurtured the inheritance and promoted its growth. In all this there are remarkable parallels with the development of the Baldwin empire.

South of the Border

James Baldwin died in 1811. In Chapter 6 it was seen how on the death of 'Father', 'Brother John' had taken over.

By 1820, under John's sound management the firm of J & J Baldwin had become the most notable spinners in the district around Halifax, known for their pioneering instincts and celebrated for their business acumen. They were innovators in the use of new machinery and the first to use steam power in the district. More important, they were well respected for their honesty and

John Baldwin, first Mayor of Halifax. His father, James, founded J. & J. Baldwin Ltd.

integrity in commercial dealings. The firm grew and prospered. Moving from its original site at Malt Shovel Yard, it acquired property, appropriately enough situated close to an area known as the 'woolshops', on the east side of Northgate in Halifax. More mills were constructed, at first in larger premises, Bailey Hall Mills at Waterside; others included Clay House Mill.

Like Alloa, the town of Halifax benefited greatly from the success of a major yarn producer. The pump priming by Baldwins gave Halifax an industrial and commercial edge over other rival centres in Yorkshire for many years to come.

Social Interests and Responsibility

Like the Paton family, the Baldwins felt they had an obligation to return something to society. John Baldwin, son of the founder of the firm, is quoted as saying 'We are sent into this world to be useful to others' and he certainly made his own contribution. A man of simple manners and of great integrity, he gained the respect and confidence of those around him. He lived at Clay House and was a popular figure throughout his life. It was said that 'his word was sure'. He was chosen to oversee the township of Halifax in 1825. At a time when the town was poorly lit and the roads were not safe, he became one of the two honorary Chief Constables. Later he was appointed a magistrate on the formation of the Halifax Borough Bench. Together with John Crossley, of carpet fame, he was responsible for the establishment of the *Halifax Courier* and they saw this through some difficult times. In addition he was a staunch Christian and a notable figure in church life.

Perhaps his greatest accolade came when, in a three-cornered contest, he was selected the first mayor of Halifax with a landslide majority; his portrait, dressed in mayoral robes and clasping a copy of the *Courier,* hangs in Halifax town hall today. He lived to the age of eighty-four.

John Baldwin's grandson, another John but referred to as J Herbert L Baldwin, who played a significant part in the management of the developing firm, also became a Mayor of Halifax. This was appropriately enough in the Golden Jubilee year of the town's incorporation in 1898 – fifty years after his grandfather had first held the position. It was J Herbert L Baldwin who was to become the first Chairman of Patons & Baldwins Limited when the two firms merged in 1920.

Innovation in Production

When Lister invented his wool combing machine in 1840, the Baldwins were one of the first companies to install it, even though they had to pay £1,000 royalties for the privilege. It was this device, perhaps more than others, which contributed to the expansion of the firm because it not only speeded up the wool combing process, which had previously proved a constraint on production, but it also improved the quality of the finished product.

To maintain quality, Baldwins used to take the pick of English, Scottish and Irish wools and, like Patons, found out that they had to go abroad in search of supplies of the right quality. Additional sources were found in Australia, South Africa, Argentina and Spain, and the skill of the firm's wool blenders was continually being put to the test to create the right 'recipe' in spinning the best yarn for their customers.

The Baldwin Beehive

At this stage, their major rivals in the quality of handknitting yarn produced in

Advertisement from 1920.

Great Britain were Patons. Baldwins jealously guarded their standards, which, as one source states, 'are admitted even by their competitors to have no superior'. For the protection of their customers and to safeguard themselves, they registered a trademark, a beehive, and 'there was no part of the civilised world in which it was not known and appreciated'. The BB, possibly originally standing for Baldwin's Beehive, but in advertisements after the merger appearing as Britain's Best, and the "Beehive" device, were registered on the 3rd May 1876 as number 5337 on the Trade Marks Registry. The Beehive word by itself was registered on 21st December 1885 under twelve different classes which received the official numbers from 49774 to 49786. On 19th May 1888 there were two further registrations: the BB which became 76418 and the BB and two bees device as 76420. It was the promulgation of the Trade Marks Act in 1875 that caused a crowding of trade mark registrations in the period shortly after — both the Baldwin Beehive and the Paton Rose having been in use well before their dates of registration. By the late nineteenth century as well as selling direct to shopkeepers throughout the United Kingdom, they had developed overseas markets; Baldwins were one of Britain's biggest textile exporters by the outbreak of the Great War in 1914 and customers could be found in all continents.

'Woolcraft' and Leaflets
Baldwins came to the same conclusions as Patons regarding the necessity of providing written instructions for knitting designs. In the early twentieth century the firm was producing illustrated pamphlets covering designs for all sorts of garments and articles. They also brought out the handknitting publication *Woolcraft,* which quickly became something of a knitter's bible. This publicaton is still produced and is now in its 21st edition, having sold millions of copies and been translated into many foreign languages.

Towards the Merger
In 1900 the decision was taken to amalgamate with a number of firms in the Yorkshire and Leicestershire areas. Essentially these comprised two important partnerships, those of John Whitmore, Son & Company, of Leicester and Melton Mowbray and the Wakefield partnerships of R H Barker & Company and Isaac Briggs & Company. Whitmores had an exceptionally high reputation for handknitting yarns, notably under their 'Cycle' trademark, and strong

Clark Bridge Mills, Halifax.

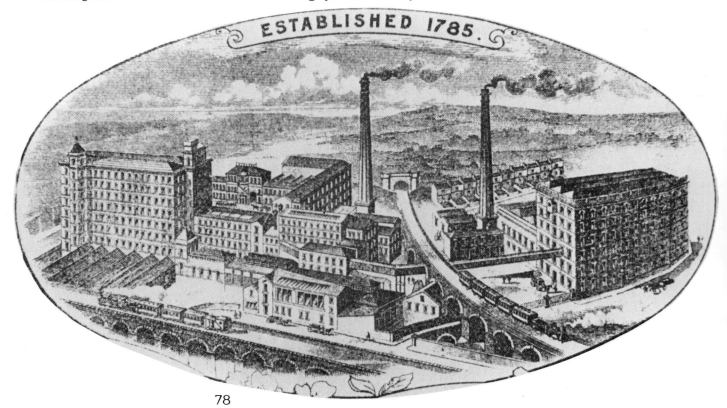

78

connections with the wholesale trade. A private limited company, J & J Baldwin and Partners Ltd, was formed with a capital of £550,000. Even then control of the new company remained firmly in the Baldwin family's hands.

Just before the merger with Patons, J & J Baldwins and Partners Ltd were sending out over 900,000 kilograms weight of yarn per month — half of this alone from the main warehouse in Halifax.

By the end of the First World War the business environment was ripe for merger. Walter Wilson, writing in the Overseas Daily Mail at the time, said 'As all know there is a tremendous outlet for all these classes of wool in the home country. With more leisure, due to the cessation of war and the shorter hours of labour, our womenfolk are devoting greater time to knitting garments. There is no limit ... The hand-made article has a characteristic of its own, and in addition there is a sense of satisfaction that the wearer gains from the knowledge that it is her own handiwork ... it is also true in regard to overseas markets'. He continues 'It is intended by both parties ... that the united firms of Patons and Baldwins Ltd shall be even more progressive ... and that such progress shall find its expression in greater output linked up with a correspondingly better service to a world-wide clientele'.

CHAPTER 9
An Industry Geared to a Pastime

The Edwardian era had seen marked shifts in attitudes, but the Great War of 1914-1918 may be considered the watershed in the major social upheavals which have characterised the twentieth century and which in turn imposed change on business.

Before 1918, financial pundits were suggesting that, since the separate entities of John Paton, Son & Co Ltd and J & J Baldwin and Partners Ltd were similar, it would be beneficial for them to pool their resources. The two firms shared many identical strengths in production and in overlapping markets, and in their attitudes towards workers and local communities.

It was recognised that there would be difficulties associated with merging — the families were still closely involved in their respective businesses. However talks were started by the directors of both firms, the financial press contrived to suggest that something was in the wind, and rumours abounded. When the official news of the merger broke there was tremendous excitement in most quarters of the textile industry, and especially amongst the workforce.

'The Commercial History of the Knitting Wool Industry'
The *Overseas Daily Mail* on 24th April 1920, said 'The commercial history of the knitting wool industry is really the story of the business of Messrs J and J Baldwin and Partners Ltd., of Halifax and of that of the equally well known Scottish business of Messrs John Paton, Son and Co Ltd., Alloa. These concerns were recently amalgamated under the style of Patons & Baldwins Ltd.' The firm's continuing impact upon and contribution to the development of the craft of handknitting since the merger cannot be doubted.

At the time Patons had three large mills and warehouses in the Alloa area and agencies in London, Manchester, Leicester, Belfast, Melbourne, Sydney and Montreal. Baldwins had three mills in Halifax and the mills connected with the businesses which had merged with Baldwins in 1900, those being in Holmfirth, Leicester, Melton Mowbray, Sowerby Bridge and Wakefield.

The Halifax mills were not immortal and have long since disappeared, and the Head Office is now in Darlington. Today the firm's production facilities are on the site of the original Kilncraigs' Mill in Alloa.

Early Board Meetings
In those early days of the merger there was a desire for equality between the two component firms, of which the allocation of Head Office and Chair-

THE BOARD OF DIRECTORS

STANDING
T. A. Waites, M. W. G. Henderson

SEATED
C. M Bell, J. C. Hawthorne, A. L. Henderson

Scottish fishermen's wives

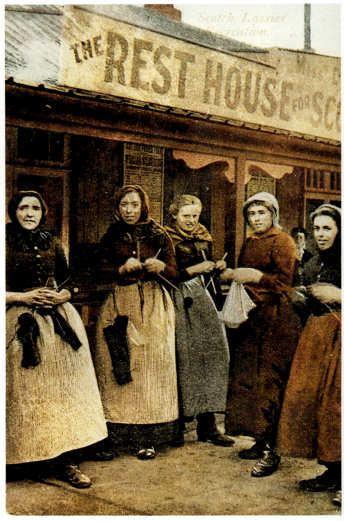

manship between Halifax and Alloa was a symptom. Where should the firm's Board meetings be held – at Halifax or Alloa? The answer – more or less midway at Carlisle! In the 1920s the status equivalent of a company aeroplane was for a firm to arrange for a special coach on a train. On the morning of the day of a Board meeting, the three Leicestershire Directors boarded a coach specially arranged by the company, and attached to one of the Midland Railway's express services. The train stopped at Leeds to pick up the four Yorkshire Directors plus the Company Secretary, together with his retinue and records. The party ate lunch on the train as the impressive scarlet coloured steam locomotive pulled it northwards through Yorkshire, and over the celebrated Settle/Appleby line onwards to Carlisle.

Meanwhile, at Stirling, the Scottish Directors and their party boarded the London express, with lunch taken as the train sped southwards through the Border country. At Carlisle, just before four o'clock the English contingent's train would arrive, and just after four the Scottish train would steam in. The fourteen directors, administrative staff, and any support management required for the meeting such as production personnel, wool buyers, or senior sales people, had arrived.

The Wider Patons and Baldwins Family
Gradually the firm welded the staff of two strong minded groups of Scottish and English workers into one. Senior staff were provided with the opportunity to visit 'the other half's' factories and sometimes people at one location were given the chance of promotion at another.

British Empire Exhibition
During the years of the amalgamation the staff were well catered for with social and sports facilities, and inter-mill events were frequently a highlight of the sporting years. Normal hours of work were forty-eight per week which included Saturday morning. Wages for girls were 18 shillings (90p) and for overlookers (foremen) £2 and 10 shillings (£2.50). At this time, rents were at 3 shillings and 6 pence (17½p) and a man's suit 50 shillings (£2.50).

The early years were not without their traumas. In February 1925, one of the local Halifax papers ran the headline 'A Thrilling Night Spectacle'. A disaster had nearly occurred when Clark Bridge Mills were ravaged by fire. The press described the vivid scenes and fierce blaze which lit the whole of Halifax with a huge red glow as if from a giant torch. Fortunately the Fire Brigade soon managed to control the blaze which appears to have been more spectacular than damaging.

The firm staged a magnificent display at the British Empire Exhibition held at London in August 1924. In the Australian Pavilion the Company took three stands. The theme presented to the visiting public was 'From Fleece to Yarn' – the wool sheared from the sheep on one stand was being turned into yarn at the stand opposite, and being made up into rugs at the third. The excitement of this event and co-operation between the mills in preparing for it, with all the resultant publicity, provided one of the stepping stones in bringing the two components of the firm closer together. This Exhibition was also probably the point where the knitting public started to accept the company as one entity.

A special excursion train was run for the Halifax workers to visit the exhibition. Some 800 boarded the train just before midnight for the tiring yet happy trip to London and the Exhibition. Arriving in London at the crack of dawn, dozens of motor char-a-bancs took the party on a trip round the sights of London before taking them on to Wembley. One of the most memorable parts of the trip involved a member of staff laying a wreath at the Cenotaph in remembrance of the many workers of the then separate Paton and Baldwin firms who had given their lives for their country during the Great War. After breakfast in restaurants in Piccadilly, the sight-seeing continued until the party eventually sat down to a roast beef luncheon in the Stadium Hall at Wembley. Then, apart from tea which had also been laid on, they were free to see the wonders of the Exhibition, from the Palaces of Engineering, Industry, Arts or Beauty to the coal mine, from the Dominion pavilions to the Queen's doll house, or the amusement park. No doubt exhausted, but still happy, the party caught a train just before midnight, for the return to Halifax. And the price — thirty shillings and three pence (£1.50)!

A Royal Visit
In July 1931 the firm had a royal visitor. Prince George, the youngest son of King George V, flew to Halifax in an open aeroplane. To fly was daring for a member of the Royal family in those days. After what was described by the press as a fine landing, the Prince was whisked away in a car through the crowded Halifax streets to Patons & Baldwins' Clark Bridge Mills. He visited the power house, the dyeing room, and saw the processes of drawing, spinning, twisting and reeling. Apparently His Royal Highness was fascinated by the way in which knitting yarns were manufactured.

After lunch at the factory a large crowd of cheering mill girls, in multi-coloured overalls which added brightness to the occasion, gave Prince George a resounding farewell.

Fourth and Fifth Generation Baldwins
When Mr Trevor Baldwin, a great-grandson of one of the founders, retired from the directorate in 1924, about a thousand people gathered to pay tribute to him at Clark Bridge Mills, Halifax. It was said that never had so many employees gathered together at one time to show their appreciation. During the presentation to him of a massive inscribed silver tray, it was said he always had a kind manner — 'in fact he was a pal rather than an employer without being too familiar'. Mr Baldwin in replying, said, amid laughter, that he had originally been brought to the mill by his father to keep him out of mischief.

In 1945 Mr J. Herbert L Baldwin died. He was a fifth generation member of the family, the last chairman of J & J Baldwin and Partners Ltd and the first of Patons & Baldwins Limited. As well as having been Halifax's youngest Mayor at the age of thirty-four, he was a strong churchman and presented St Jude's church with a stained glass window in memory of his father and gave a hall to the village of Lockton. Mr Baldwin was also prominent in the town's commercial life, being sometime Chairman of the Chamber of Commerce as well as a Justice of the Peace and holding many other offices.

Later Members of the Patons Family
The involvement of the Patons line in the firm continued into the 1950s.

William T. Proctor was Chairman of the Company from 1924 until 1938. He was the son of the granddaughter of the original John Paton. As a young man he had joined his father in John Paton, Son & Company and gained a practical knowledge of all stages in the production of yarn. He became a partner in the firm and the first Chairman when it became a Private Limited Company. On amalgamation with Baldwins he became vice Chairman and in 1924 Chairman of Patons & Baldwins Limited. The Alloa Advertiser on his death in 1938 wrote 'Under his shrewd direction and dynamic leadership the company extended its operations by acquiring further interests in England, Canada, Australia, China and USA. New factories were built in Toronto, Canada; Launceston, Tasmania; and Shanghai, China while substantial additions to the factories were built in Alloa and Halifax. The Share and Debenture issues which were increased to finance these ventures were so successful that the capital remains a first class security. In business acumen he was almost unerring, quick to see the advantages of any project and trenchant in criticism of weakness'.

Although it continued that 'His work was his hobby', William Proctor nevertheless found time to follow the family's tradition of service to the community. Amongst many offices, he was a manager of the County Accidents Hospital and Chairman of the Board of Management for several years.

William Proctor had connections with the Company for 59 years and after he died in 1938 another member of the Patons family, Alexander Forrester-Paton became Chairman until 1951.

The Inter-War Period
During the inter-war period, the firm continued its consolidation into one entity. Major contributions to its development during that period on the overseas front are dealt with in Chapter 10, 'Patons Around the World'.

The Move to Darlington
After the Second World War it became clear that the firm would need to expand its production capacity in the United Kingdom. The firm would have liked to have maintained its English roots in its home areas but it had become increasingly clear that most of the English mills were not suitable for the latest machinery that had been developed, and which would have to be installed if the firm were to be competitive. They were also too scattered.

Of the options open, one was to knock down one of the Halifax mills and to rebuild. This was not viable because no single site owned by the firm in Halifax was large enough. Where could a site of at least the hundred acres required, together with a good supply of labour and water be found?

Discussions were held with the Government, especially concerning labour availability and priorities for development areas. After feasibility studies during 1944 and 1945, a decision was taken to move the major English production facilities to Darlington. As remarkable as the speed of execution of the move was the extent of the development itself.

Helped by the level surface of the 140-acre site, (half the size of Hyde Park), building commenced during February 1946: twenty months later the first spinning machines were installed and within two years of cutting the first turf the manufacturing of yarn began in January 1948. The company had had a difficult decision to make. The war had developed technology in many areas, but textile machinery had taken a back seat. One machine alone had reached a modest scale trials stage, the centrifugal spinner of Prince Smith and Stells, which ran at nearly twice the speeds enjoyed hitherto. The Darlington concept was heavily dependant on innovation, and here was a potential production revolution. A gamble was taken and a large installation ordered. Alas! the gamble did not come off and these spinning machines had to be replaced at

The main Spinning Shed in the Darlington mill covered an area of thirteen acres.

the end of the 1950s by the new apron spinners. By 1951, 34 acres had been covered with buildings, and to build these over 14 million bricks had been used, together with nearly 18 million kilograms of steel and over 90 thousand litres of paint. Apart from the office block, with its magnificent foyer, the mill was entirely a series of one-storey buildings to permit the efficient flow of yarn through the various production processes.

Other statistics were equally impressive: raw wool was conveyed by air suction to a nearby shed which was over 300 metres long and housed forty-four carding machines; over 650 thousand cubic metres of space inside the mill was air-conditioned; the power house could produce enough electricity to light a small town and was linked to the National Grid; over 6 million kilograms of knitting yarn per annum could be produced by the plant; the factory was also a major producer of hosiery yarn used by knitwear manufacturers; there was a canteen with seats for 1,500 people which doubled as a theatre having a fully equipped stage and dressing rooms. As well as eighteen tea counters to serve up to 160 people each, there were 50 acres of sports grounds for staff, including football and cricket pitches.

Work on the Darlington plant commenced in 1946; the manufacture of yarn began in 1948. This mill was the showpiece of the British textile industry.

Philip Wright

Both the Patons and Baldwins enterprises had acquired numerous firms since their individual foundation and this process continued after the firm's amalgamation. In 1908 J & J Baldwin and Partners Ltd took over the Wakefield firm of R H Barker and Co Ltd, one of the Directors of which was a Mr F H Wright. In the grounds of the Barker millhouse at Thornes near Wakefield, his son Philip Arton Wright was born in 1885. This millhouse was still in use with successor firms until well into the twentieth century.

After comprehensive training and a distinguished career in the Great War, in 1923 he succeeded his father as one of the now Patons & Baldwins Limited's Directors. He saw the great overseas developments. By the Second World War the Board recognised that changing technology and markets did not lend themselves to old and obsolete production facilities in small mills. In the middle of the 1940s, Philip Wright and his fellow Directors saw the need for the English production facilities to be relocated. Becoming Vice Chairman in 1945, he was given the responsibility to establish a modern Patons factory at Darlington.

It was said that he was not merely a figurehead since he still went on his daily rounds of the factory, always having a smile or a kind word to say to employees he passed. Nor did he forget that yarn retailers were the lifeblood

Raw wool bales in store.

of the Company and essential to its survival. Many a small woolshop owner visiting the Darlington mill during its early days was surprised to be greeted, at the then showpiece of the British textile industry, by the man whom they later found out was the Company's Chairman.

In 1951 he became Chairman of the company, completing fifty-six years service with the Company before retiring in 1959. His fellow directors commissioned Sir Gerald Kelly R.A. to paint his portrait, which hangs in the Boardroom. It can be said that Philip Wright was the father of the Darlington mill which brought the Company's English production facilities on to one site.

Excursion into Retailing

In 1960 the company obtained a substantial interest in Fleming, Reid (Greenock) Ltd and with it ownership of the chain of Scotch Wool Shops, and in 1966 the Bellman shops were acquired and integrated with the Scotch Wool Shop chain. At one time the Company had nearly 400 woolshops. After a number of years however it was felt that these did not fit into its pattern as a knitting yarn spinner and the company disposed of them, some being utilised elsewhere within the Coats Patons group.

Design and Fashion

Since the merger of Patons with Baldwins in 1920 the combined Company has put much effort into the development of knitting designs, both on the classic and fashion front. The good features from Paton's *Universal Knitting Book* were soon integrated into Baldwin's *Woolcraft*.

The standard of the design has continually been improved and the Company has operated a design department since the late 1940s, now also having design centres in its many overseas associate companies. The first colour leaflet was introduced in the 1930s and in 1932 the firm brought out the fashion knits magazine *Stitchcraft* which was soon to be selling over a quarter of a million copies each month. For fifty years, until June 1982, Stitchcraft was produced on a monthly basis, when it was turned into bi-monthy collections of specific designs.

The firm spins fashion yarns in natural fibres such as wool, mohair, angora, and the synthetic fibres acrylic and nylon, amongst others. It also produces spectacular shade ranges, which were quite enormous in the 1930s, when the combinations of self shades, marls and mixtures ran well into four figures. Patons & Baldwins have ensured that the fabrics knitted from their yarns have a high surface interest, both as far as texture and colour are concerned.

The firm has adapted to the changing requirements of knitters. It has continued to make great contributions to the popularity of knitting since the 1950s, through the many fashions in designs they have pioneered. Although fashionable designs were produced before that time, the majority of knitters merely wanted to make economical, basic garments. It was about 1950 that the firm employed James Norbury, who became, possibly, the great handknitting designer of the twentieth century. The fresh wind of fashion was blowing, design was changing, colours were being mixed.

Coats Patons

In Paisley in 1830, James and Peter Coats purchased from their father a small thread-making mill. Within a decade J & P Coats Ltd had expanded and much of its production was exported to America. Another member of the family, Andrew Coats, was sent to manage the business there. In 1896 Clark's, another thread manufacturer, merged with Coats.

The members of the families, like the Paton family in Alloa and the Baldwin family in Halifax, showed concern for their employees and local community. Working conditions were maintained at a very high standard, and in the 1880s the firm built houses for employees, hostels were made available for female workers and a community with medical and fire services established. The firm built schools, and was instrumental in the building of Paisley Technical College. With its headquarters now in Glasgow and producing complementary needlecraft products to Patons & Baldwins Limited, also sold on a worldwide basis, there were sound reasons for J & P Coats Ltd to get together with Patons & Baldwins Limited. In 1961 a merger of these two giants of the textile world took place and the firm, soon to become Coats Patons Ltd, was formed. Together the merged organisation operates fifty factories in twenty-five countries where some 40,000 people of many nationalities are employed.

The Importance of Retailers

Patons & Baldwins Limited have always appreciated the importance of retail distribution to the knitting yarn industry, realising that the spinner cannot exist

The Carding Shed at the Darlington mill was over three hundred metres long and housed forty-four carding machines.

Kilncraigs Mill, Alloa.

without outlets for the yarn produced to go through to the knitter, whether these be woolshops or yarn departments in stores. Patons have always encouraged co-operation between themselves and the yarn retailer through maintaining a well-trained sales force. They regularly take stands at major trade shows where many retailers congregate, these stands always attracting attention. Eye-catching point-of-sale material and show cards are regularly updated. Regular advertisements have appeared in various publications since the 1900s, especially women's magazines, but retailers are also helped with their local promotions which may include local advertising, fashion shows, competitions or sponsored knit-ins to raise money for charities and disasters.

In the 1970s, Patons introduced training courses for retailers, which cover such areas as product knowledge, selling and various aspects of running a woolshop or yarn department. To date over 100 of these courses have been held and attended by over 3,000 retailers.

The Last Decade

After some twenty-five years of producing both handknitting and hosiery yarns at Darlington and many other factories, it was decided in 1976 that to remain competitive in an aggressive market further reorganisation was necessary. The firm transferred all the hosiery yarn manufacture to other companies within the group and reorganised the Darlington site as the headquarters of the knitting yarn division, with production being split between Alloa, Darlington, Greenock and Wakefield.

To bring the story up to date, although the firm's headquarters had been established at Darlington, to enable production facilities to be modernised further, it was announced in 1980 that knitting yarn production would be concentrated on the Kilncraigs Mill at Alloa. There was to be an investment of over £6,500,000 to re-equip the factory with the latest machinery. To mark this, the Secretary of State for Scotland The Rt Hon George Younger MP visited the mill and said that although the textile industry was facing difficult times, Patons & Baldwins Limited had embarked upon major rationalisation and new investment because they were aware of the need to be competitive. Today, Patons & Baldwins Limited has the largest handknitting manufacturing capacity in the United Kingdom with about a quarter of their production being exported.

CHAPTER 10
Patons Around the World

Patons has played a significant role in establishing handknitting as an important leisure pursuit in many parts of the world, and has promoted the craft of knitting by the sale of knitting leaflets and yarns in many countries. It has additionally expanded its production facilities to cope with the ever-growing demand, and operating today are major Patons & Baldwins factories in Australia and Canada with an interest in a South African company.

The date when the two component firms of Patons and Baldwins first began to sell their knitting yarns abroad has not been recorded. Yet it is known that both firms were making purchases of wool from Australia and the South American countries over a hundred years ago. Just as raw wool came over the Atlantic and Pacific trade routes in the famous clipper ships, so handknitting yarns were in time sent back on the same routes. These tall ships competed fiercely in some famous races to be first home. The record time from Sydney to London was held by the famous Cutty Sark, now moored at Greenwich, which on its wool passage in 1889/90 covered the 22,500 kilometres in 75 days.

When the merger of Patons and Baldwins took place in 1920 Patons had agencies in Melbourne and Sydney in Australia, Montreal and British Columbia in Canada and in several other places. As for Baldwins, Walter Wilson wrote that 'few businesses in the textile trade have a larger clientele in overseas markets' than they did, continuing that shipments went to 'India, China, the Dominions and the Continent of Europe'.

Yet the really exciting developments overseas occurred just after the amalgamation of the two firms, during the inter-war period. In those halcyon days the now Patons & Baldwins Limited were helping to spread the craft of handknitting further afield and promoting their name to worldwide renown.

Down Under
Australia
Most people, if asked the home of sheep and wool production, would be prompt to answer: Australia. Of course, the raising of sheep for their fleeces has been going on in the Middle East since time immemorial and Europe has seen a thriving wool trade also. However, since the colonisation of Australia in the last century, the introduction of Spanish and English sheep stocks to the continent has met with remarkable success. Botany Bay has given its name to the finest merino wool, botany wool.

The mill at Launceston, Tasmania.

Launceston, Tasmania – the early days.

The Leap South
Tasmania

Tasmania is often regarded as being more British than the 'mother country', but it is very definitely part of the Australian Commonwealth, separated by only some two hundred and forty kilometres of shallow sea from the mainland. Like south-west England the climate is temperate – cold in winter and pleasantly warm in summer. The lands are fertile and provide excellent potential for manufacturing sites.

In 1923 Patons & Baldwins Limited opened a factory at Launceston, Tasmania to supply the firm's growing markets in Australia and New Zealand. Contemporary reports in the Australian press stated that Patons & Baldwins Limited were putting their resources, skill, immense capital and reputation behind the Tasmanian plant. Although the size of the plant was vast even by Australian standards, it should be remembered that at least eight of the firm's British mills were larger than the Launceston site.

The mill initially covered four and a half acres, the building had floor space of over 18,500 square metres and it is recorded that it contained fifty-five

lavatories! The main source of power was hydro-electric. And for all this, the bill came to £100,000.

The factory had the most up-to-date dyeing facilities of any textile unit in Australia in the 1920s. This enabled new shades to be launched on the market which nobody else had attempted to produce in that continent.

Scottish Immigrants

A problem at the outset was that the local people simply did not have the skills necessary to run and operate a complex textile mill. So the company asked for volunteers to go from its British factories to help in the initial stages of operating the mill and to train indigenous Tasmanians who would provide the bulk of the workforce. Mr A R Procter, a descendant of the family partners, went out with the first group and became manager.

Wednesday, 25th April 1923 was a red letter day for many of the people of Alloa, for this was the start of a great adventure in setting out for Launceston. The day of their departure saw friends and relations converging on Alloa station to bid an emotional goodbye at the first stage of a long and arduous journey.

Over the years the firm has extended its activities in Australia, including the establishment of premises on the mainland. In 1970 Coats Patons Ltd reached an agreement with Bond's Industries Ltd of Camperdown in New South Wales to merge the two firms' Australian interests, and so become the largest textile business in Australia.

The Far North
Canada

Canada's wide diversity includes its geography, its fauna and flora and its extremes in climate. The early settlers of Canada were French and British, many of the latter being Scots. Both elements brought strong knitting traditions with them to the new country. The harsh winter climate required substantial clothing.

Over the years the country's knitters have developed a particular tradition of using very thick yarns to produce bulky jackets which feature distinctive stitch patterns. Canadian traditional patterns can be divided into geometrical designs, often echoing a Nordic influence and picture knitting, sometimes depicting local scenes, or of winter sports. For these the instructions are presented in chart form, showing the French influence at work.

In Newfoundland the European settlers grew wool which they washed, carded, spun and usually bleached off-white before knitting up the yarn produced into gloves, hats, scarves, socks and sweaters. The spinning and knitting carried out by family or neighbourhood groups were referred to as *Knitting Pallies*. The fact that many of the Newfoundland outposts were settled by people from Jersey may account for some of the knitting traditions handed down, and the phrase 'Putting on your Guernsey' was often used. Hilda Chaulk Murray writes about the early days of settlement '... nearly all the girls could knit by the time they were seven or eight years old, and most of them had started at four or five years of age ... In Elliston, one of the complicated items a girl would be expected to knit, ... was a pair of long stockings for herself, or, perhaps a 'splitting mitt' for her father'. Knitting by Canadian Indians was not indigenous, but passed on to them. Ryan Brothers writes 'When the first handful of shrewd, Scottish settlers arrived in the fertile, mist-covered Cowichan Valley of southern Vancouver Island in the 19th

A Cowichan knitter.

century, they brought with them an unusual skill. By the flickering light of oil lamps, these rugged men of Scotland and the northern isles patiently sat knitting to while away the long winter nights. In time, they passed this skill on to the Indian women among whom they lived'. He continues that this skill was used as a basis of a thriving cottage industry and 'Cowichan women were soon turning out a sweater which quickly caught the eye of the white man. It kept its owner warm and dry in the coldest wind and rain, and stoutly resisted wear'.

Land of Plenty

A major market with close links with Halifax was British Columbia. But it was far removed from the primary centres of population and so remained a semi-autonomous area of the firm's activity until World War II, under a celebrated agent, Duncan Carmichael. Over 3,250 kilometres to the east, on the shores of Lake Ontario, stands Canada's second largest city, Toronto – the name originally being translated as land of plenty but today the more popular theory is that it means tree, or trees in water. Until the tumult of the Second

The Toronto mill.

World War the population of the city was predominantly British in origin and many British traditions had been maintained there.

A Yorkshire emigrant, Thomas O. Aked, started a yarn spinning firm in the outskirts of Toronto. Thomas Aked was born in 1876 in Yorkshire, England. In 1909 he went to Canada as a salesman for an English firm and later became manager for the Monarch Knitting Company. In 1918 he formed Aked & Company Ltd with a factory in Toronto producing fancy handknitting yarns. Thomas Aked is credited with having wound the first ball of knitting wool made in Canada. He was also the inventor of the Aked Prince Smith Flyer Doffer spinning machine in 1911 which revolutionised this type of spinning. The firm's success and growth continued. In 1928 it was acquired by Patons & Baldwins and was later relocated to a larger site within the city to enable production to keep pace with growing demand. Patons & Baldwins Canada Incorporated was formed at the end of 1963.

The Inscrutable Orient
China

In such a vast country as China the geography is as diverse as the peoples and dialects. With most of its land mass subject to temperate or even colder

Fair Isle caps

Sleeveless pullover 1934

The Nineteen-Fifties

climatic conditions, China provides an ideal market for handknitting yarns — although the Chinese have only recently become exponents of the craft when they learned it from Westerners. It is interesting to note that many Chinese still knit from patterns learnt by heart.

In the 1900s it was the Baldwin company that first saw the potential of this market. They developed trade through European merchant houses in China and their agents in London, Manchester and Hamburg. The key centre was Shanghai, near the mouth of that great trading artery the Yangtze river.

In the 1920s the newly merged Company decided to open a Shanghai sales office to provide closer and direct contact with the China market. As the market developed a Mill was built in 1931.

English Immigrants

Although Shanghai had the benefit of an indigenous textile industry, there was a shortage of local labour capable of supervising the new plant. As in the Tasmanian situation, a British workforce had to be formed to provide these skills. This time recruitment was mostly in the West Riding of Yorkshire, 60% of the people concerned coming from Patons' Wakefield mill.

The new factory employed some 850 persons with a maximum capacity of over two and a quarter million kilograms weight of yarn annually, primarily for handknittings but also for machine knitting and weaving purposes. Sales were given a boost by the erection of an enormous illuminated neon sign in the very centre of Shanghai's busiest streets. This sign towered above the

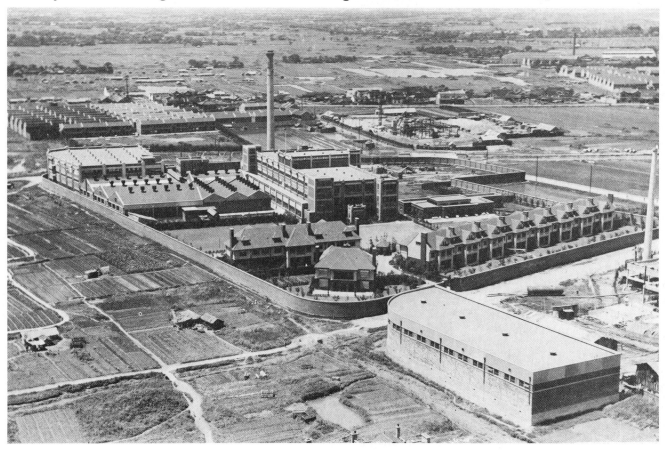

The Shanghai mill.

In the centre of Shanghai, a neon sign proclaims its message.

surrounding buildings. As the bees flew round and round the hive it declared to all who watched that Beehive knitting wools – BRITAIN'S BEST – were now established on Chinese soil.

The Last Days in China

As the Second World War erupted in Europe in 1939 with repercussions in the Far East, some of the families were evacuated, but the remaining Patons staff were interned for the duration. After four difficult years of war, peace was restored and the mill was repossessed by Patons staff.

Nevertheless the writing was on the wall for British operations in Shanghai. The Chinese Nationalists were in trouble and the Communists were gaining in strength and confidence from day to day.

It was decided that the firm would hold on in Shanghai for as long as possible.

In 1949 the Communist army captured Shanghai. The Yorkshire Post cabled a message of concern and encouragement which was answered "staff cheerful, unruffled." Patons was the penultimate foreign firm to leave Chinese soil. In 1958 the Shanghai mill was taken over by a Communist-sponsored buyer, and the remaining British staff returned home.

Today, the factory built by Patons still produces knitting yarn for China's teeming population which now nears one billion. However the mill is now under Communist control.

Another Crock of Gold
South Africa

Africa presents another continent of wide contrasts, ranging from the deserts in the north with intolerably dry heat, through the jungles and bush of central Africa, to the more temperate climate of the south. Surprisingly, despite the heat, knitting is carried out in many parts of Africa – there are wool shops in many places including Nairobi, which is near the Equator!

Patons has exported knitting wool to Africa from pre-merger times. The African market was much smaller than the Chinese, but 90,000 kilograms weight of yarns were being sent to South Africa in the 1950s. Increasing protectionism and exchange controls were likely to affect Patons' position there.

One local mill which spun hosiery yarns, Randfontein Textiles (SA) based in Randfontein west of Johannesburg was owned by P and J Tiberghien of Tourcoing, France. A new company, Patons & Baldwins (South Africa) Pty with a 50% ownership was formed to take over and run the factory. Machinery to spin handknitting yarn was installed.

The World is Their Oyster

In addition to the overseas units manufacturing Patons & Baldwins yarns, the company sells its products in over one hundred countries, including Abu Dhabi, Austria, Barbados, Belgium, Canada, Cyprus, Denmark, Dominican Republic, Dubai, Falkland Islands, Finland, France, Gibraltar, Greece, Grenada, Holland, Hong Kong, Italy, Ireland, Japan, Jordan, Korea, Kuwait, Madeira, Malaysia, Mauritius, Nepal, Norway, Qatar, Singapore, South Africa, Sweden, Switzerland, Trinidad, and the United States of America – through many agents, large trading houses such as Jardine Matheson in the Far East, and associated Coats Patons Group Companies in many parts of the world several of which also manufacture handknitting yarns.

CHAPTER 11
Around the Coastline

Before examining Patons' role in stimulating knitting as a high-fashion craft in Britain, it would be appropriate to examine in the next two chapters the local traditions in coastal communities, which have had such an effect on fashion in knitwear.

Although Great Britain is a comparatively small island, it has an extensive coastline, dotted with tiny fishing harbours like Polperro in Cornwall or beaches like Winterton-on-Sea in Norfolk, as well as major fishing ports such as Aberdeen and Hull. Whatever their scale of activities today, many of the traditions of fishermen within them can be traced to the same roots, the hardships and hazards of a living earned from the sea. The elements have played their part in producing a close community spirit and a breed of hardy men, with families forever conscious that a quirk of nature could rob them of a loved one.

Comfort and Warmth

There can be no doubt that knitting has played an important part in creating clothing for seamen and fishermen for at least two hundred years, yet it is only recently that local historians have recorded the contributions of the fishing communities to the craft. The Channel Islands of Jersey and Guernsey have given their names to two similar, yet distinct, jumper-type garments. Everybody must have had a jersey at some time or another, but until recently relatively few mainland people had heard of the guernsey or gansey, both the spelling and pronunciation of which varies in different localities.

Fishermen require warm garments to protect them from both cold and wet and in such a hazardous and arduous occupation they also need to be able to move easily and react quickly to avoid possible dangers and cannot afford to be hampered by restrictive clothing. The traditional gansey meets these requirements by being protective, for it is virtually waterproof, and also by providing warmth and considerable freedom of movement. These qualities were soon appreciated by fishermen all over Britain.

Wool – The Ideal Yarn

Wool is a natural insulating material which, when matted into an oil thatch on the backs of sheep, protects them from the worst privations of British mountain winters. Each individual fibre has overlapping scales along its surface which help the fibres interlock, trapping air between them, and either

by using the yarn oiled with natural lanolin from the sheep, or by knitting the gansey on finer needles than usual to create a firm fabric, wool's natural properties of wind and water resistance can be exploited to the full.

The effective insulating nature of wool also means that a certain amount of water can be absorbed by a garment without the wearer feeling damp and uncomfortable.

Badge of Identity

Generally the women of each fishing community produced ganseys which, whilst not identical to each other, were readily recognisable as coming from that locality. Variations in pattern formations were common between families, and sometimes within families, as the menfolk married and other traditions were brought in.

In addition to each gansey being identifiable as having been produced in a certain community, the wearer's initials or full name could be knitted in purl stitches on the plain portion of the gansey above the welt, to assist in identification should the fisherman be drowned and his otherwise unrecognisable body be later washed ashore.

Whilst certain pattern formations may have been indicative of specific communities, there is some evidence to show that patterns travelled along the coast when fishermen from the Scottish fleets called into fishing ports along the coasts of North East of England and East Anglia, or when the prospect of good fishing called the fishermen of England northwards.

Perhaps one contribution to the exchange of ideas was that the young women who were employed at herring gutting and salting would follow the fish for employment. These women spent spare moments knitting and the different ganseys worn by the locals in the ports they travelled to would have influenced their own efforts.

However, the patterns on ganseys in some areas became so distinctive that at the fishing fairs held in many Yorkshire coastal villages, the experienced onlooker could tell from which part of the country a fisherman was likely to come from by the style of gansey he wore. Stitch patterns from Filey, Flamborough, Robin Hood's Bay, Scarborough, Staithes and Whitby were quite readily identifiable to an expert.

Knitting the Gansey

Ganseys were not only warm and practical garments. Both the knitter and the wearer were proud of the workmanship involved and young girls would start to knit early in life as it was considered productive and necessary employment, to be fitted in whenever the chores allowed. Occasionally gansey knitting was used to supplement the family income but this was on a small and local scale, the demand coming mainly form fishermen who did not have a woman to knit for them.

Ganseys from the Channel Islands and the ports along the coasts of England and Scotland were commonly knitted in the round on sets of five or more fine needles to make a smooth, firm fabric. The wool, usually the equivalent thickness of today's 4-ply yarns, was, however, often made up of 5 or 6 strands of worsted spun wool, plied together to give a very smooth hard wearing yarn. The colour was commonly navy, sometimes black. Ancient ganseys in mid-grey-blue are usually faded to that colour by wind and sea!

Ganseys were fairly square in shape. The body of the garment was started

The traditional seal-skin cap and gansey handknitted in the "Larner" family pattern.

Scottish fishermen's wives. The girls standing 2nd and 4th from the left, back row, are wearing knitting belts.

either in ribbing or garter stitch using 2 strands of yarn for added strength, and usually from between one quarter to two-thirds of the body was knitted plain, the remainder being worked in the distinctive combinations of purled stitches, ridges and cables according to the knitter's preference and the tradition of the area. However some ganseys were worked completely plain while others were started in pattern almost immediately after the welt.

Until relatively recently there were no written instructions; pattern stitches and garment designs were handed down by word of mouth, whilst individual fit was achieved by experience, a keen eye and perhaps a tape measure.

The gansey was worked in the round up to the armholes where the stitches for the back and front were divided and the remainder of the body was worked on 2 needles, a gusset having first been worked at the underarm to allow ease of movement in an otherwise snug fitting garment. The stand up neck was traditionally tight fitting, to keep out the wind, though neck scarves were often worn, and in Scotland was occasionally buttoned to allow for a closer fit. Sleeves were picked up in the round at the armhole and knitted downwards and were mostly quite short, ending 10 to 12mm up from the wrist so that they were out of the way when the fishermen were working. Knitting the sleeves down from the body had a practical advantage since they could easily be unravelled and re-worked when cuffs or elbows wore out. By working the gansey in this manner, seams were virtually avoided.

Knitters would often arrange for the wearer to have fitting sessions at appropriate stages in the progress of their knitting. There may have been three or four such fittings, perhaps one at the division of the arms, the next when the neck was to be completed, and the last when the length of sleeve was to be finalised. This lead to an improved fit. To facilitate the knitting of ganseys, the knitters would use sheaths similar to those described in Chapter 5.

The knitting also took on a social role. In summer, gansey knittters would be found congregating on the beach, waiting for the boats to return, and taking their knitting with them. They would chat and gossip with their friends, and sometimes there would be a sing song. When the boats arrived the women would help unload the catch and then perhaps gut the fish. During the winter, the gansey knitters would join their friends and neighbours in one anothers' houses, especially if they were outworkers for a merchant in a nearby town. Talking and knitting together there was a good deal of friendly (and sometimes not so friendly!) rivalry over speed and craftmanship.

The Romance of the Gansey
The everyday gansey was a knitted equivalent of the inland woven smock and just as farm workers had more intricate smocks for high days and holidays so the knitting of bridal shirts with symbolic stitch patterns such as marriage lines was traditional in most coastal areas.

James Norbury, had a delightful anecdote about the tradition of knitting bridal shirts. In some of the Cornish fishing ports, when a lass was courting a fisherman, she would set about making a special gansey for her betrothed. It

would be both elaborate and beautiful, using a combination of traditional stitches from both their villages or families. Produced as a token of their future union, it would be worn by the bridegroom on his wedding day and kept thereafter for special occasions.

In the Cornish village of Polperro, the ganseys were referred to as knit-frocks. The village choir, largely composed of fishermen, used to wear these when they sang. Photographs taken in mid-nineteenth century of the Revered Robert Hawker in the village of Morwenstow – who was a very good poet and appears to have been a bit of an eccentric – show him wearing a fisherman's jersey under a three-quarter length coat, instead of the conventional clothes of a cleric. He did so because he said it showed him to be a 'fisher of men'.

The Stitch Patterns

The individual stitch patterns to be found in traditional ganseys were generally passed down from mother to daughter. New stitch patterns evolved either by accident or ingenuity but the placing and combination of a quite limited number of individual designs lead to a wealth of diverse gansey designs which nonetheless were linked by the similarities of the components.

The name given to the stitches would tell of the fisherman's tools of trade, his harvest from the sea, the environment in which he worked and the

Scottish fishermen in their ganseys. This illustrates the individual stitch patterns which were used.

weather he endured. Thus ladders became the rig, cables the coils of rope and diamonds reflected the shape of mesh fishing nets. Sometimes anchors or flags appeared to provide extra embellishment. Herringbone patterns would be interpreted as depicting the harvest from the sea and purl ridges on stocking stitch were known as Ridge and Furrow.

The Cottage Industry

Gansey knitting became a cottage industry in the small fishing villages near the larger ports. For example Scottish gansey knitters would supply the town of Fraserburgh, those of Yorkshire would supply Hull and on the Norfolk coast there was demand from Great Yarmouth. In the case of the latter, villagers from Caister-on-Sea, Winterton-on-Sea and other nearby villages would knit on an out-worker basis. A firm in Great Yarmouth, Johnson's, would supply wool to their knitters in outlying districts and collect the finished product at a later date. The firm sent a pony and trap six miles to Winterton-on-Sea each month, to a cottage in the village which was the central distribution and collection point. A postcard would have been sent to warn of the date of the visit and some thirty out-workers would arrive with their work for which they received payment and then would collect a new batch of yarn to knit up during the coming month.

Approximately 26 ozs (800 grams) of yarn went into a gansey and in 1900 the payment was about 4 shillings (20p) for the finished article. It was recognised that a competent knitter could earn about 10 shillings (50p) for a month's work.

The Death Knell of the Gansey

The gansey was a special garment for many reasons. In addition to its economic and practical advantages, it had an aesthetic and social function. As well as enabling the fisherman to be more effective in his job, the practice of gathering in groups, either on the beach or in each others' house, encouraged comradeship and healthy competition amongst the women of the village. Until recently, the word gansey, meaning a particular form of knitted garment, had virtually ceased to be in common usage, even in previously strong fishing communities.

In the late 1930s, Gladys Thompson, in her *Guernsey and Jersey Patterns*, writes that she sent a group of fishermen dolls she had made to the National Federation of Women's Institutes Exhibition in London in 1938. Two were of fisherwomen, one of whom was knitting a tiny gansey, and four of the fishermen wearing different patterned Yorkshire guernseys. She writes 'Queen Elizabeth (The Queen Mother) saw them and asked me their history'. It has recently seen some revival due to the interest created by research into this craft from about the 1950s. In retrospect it seems inevitable that gansey knitting would decline like so many other rural crafts. Industrialisation enabled mass production of cheaper but inferior garments. At the same time the introduction of larger fishing vessels operating from a few major ports meant the decline and even extinction of the small fishing communities.

By the time the twentieth century dawned, ganseys were being made in quantity by machine and today their individual identity has become confused with other sweater styles worn by the modern fisherman. The decline was accelerated by the fact that as older men in the small fishing villages retired, fewer sons took their place – the youngsters had gone into towns to earn a better living outside the fishing industry. Women began to take local factory,

Cornish fishermen.

shop or office jobs which were easier and far more remunerative than gansey knitting. Mothers no longer taught their daughters how to carry out the craft and today it has become a rarity to find someone who can knit the traditional gansey. Fortunately there has recently been some interest in garments reminiscent of the traditional gansey in style. These are designed with a looser stitch tension to make them easier to knit and are now often made in the flat rather than the round, but nevertheless provide a valuable reminder of a once grand tradition.

CHAPTER 12
The Island Knitters

The importance of fishermen in the development of the superb craft of knitting ganseys has been touched upon in the previous chapter. However, this is not the whole story, for knitting has laid down its own special traditions on some islands and these are probably some of the best known today.

Most people are familiar with the sweaters knitted using Aran, Shetland and Fair Isle designs and patterns; although not related to the production of fishermen's garments, the Shetland Islanders' tradition of lace knitting is also worthy of consideration.

Knitting while on the move was not a problem for the island knitters. Yarn was often spun while afloat.

On the islands, as with gansey knitting elsewhere, traditional local stitch patterns and designs developed among their fishing communities. Fair Isle and Shetland sweaters soon became immediately recognisable and the combination of cultural influences and the skill of knitters in the area encouraged the evolution of the distinctive style so well loved today.

In the nineteenth century knitting reached its peak in the islands, in terms of the level of craftmanship and amount of work being produced.

To the West of Ireland
Aran

The Aran Islands are to be found in Galway Bay off the west coast of Ireland. Exposure to the Atlantic gales has given these islands a rugged beauty, and the climate has in turn produced a breed of hardy people. Generations of islanders have faced a harsh, frugal life, drawing a meagre crop from the poor soil in a bleak terrain and wresting an existence from the often cruel sea.

The number of people living on the islands has varied in response to the strength of the local economy and America welcomed many of the islanders when she accepted the masses of European emigrants in the last century. Today, the population has dwindled, but the islanders who remain are an independent and dignified people.

The islands' fishermen, who faced the rough seas and harsh weather in their small boats, called curraghs, needed clothing which would keep them dry and warm and the Aran gansey met these requirements admirably.

The Aran Shirt

In the islands the garment knitted was usually referred to as a shirt or a sea shirt. The hardy sheep produced a fibre which was spun into a thickish, rough yarn and left part oiled. Its natural creamy colour was called bainin and is the traditional colour of Aran shirts.

The garment would be made in stitches and patterns that had the effect of sculptured relief, such as diamonds, cables and zig-zags, creating a thick weatherproof fabric. Many Aran stitch patterns, some of which carry Celtic symbols pre-dating the Christian era or Viking, have been recorded by Heinz Edgar Kiewe. They include the basics of cables and honeycombs, but also a range of symbolic designs, often religious, which he has tried to explain. Among them are the tree or ladder of life, leading upwards to heaven after a virtuous life; the trellis, indicating man's bond with God; and Trinity stitch for the Holy Trinity, the three in one. He also mentions spoon stitch, the lover's pattern, and marriage lines, a double zig-zag that represents the wedded couple's life running in constant parallel, but with ups and downs! Other popular stitches in Aran garments include blackberry stitch, the fern, basket stitch, the claw and the sea-horse stitch. It is interesting to note that some authentic Aran ganseys have horizontal bands of pattern, but though there are many variations in complexity and stitch arrangement, traditional Aran design has a unique and distinct flavour.

To the North of Scotland
The Shetlands

The Shetlands consist of a group of some one hundred islands, about a hundred and fifty miles north of the Scottish mainland, twenty of which are inhabited. This barren and windswept area was occupied by the Vikings in the seventh and eighth centuries, and eventually settled by Norwegians during

A fine example of an Aran sweater.

the ninth and tenth. For years since, Lerwick – the main town and port – has been a centre of the sea routes from the Baltic and the North Sea to Iceland and the Atlantic.

The Shetland tradition of knitting goes back many centuries and hand knitted hose were once a staple export of the islands, with production reaching a peak in the seventeenth- and eighteenth-centuries. There followed a period of decline for the industry, which picked up again in the middle of the nineteenth century when the islands' products were firmly established by a London merchant, Edward Stanton. To help promote interest in the islands' hosiery knitters, one Arthur Anderson presented Queen Victoria with a pair of Shetland knitted stockings in 1837.

Knitting was carried out by crofters to help eke out their subsistence living from the land and sea. The women would help on the croft, especially feeding cattle and poultry, and when time allowed would knit as they walked about.

The islands' knitters developed two distinct traditions; one is the knitting of Shetland sweaters which are less colourful than their Fair Isle counterparts, the other is the startling contrast of lace knitting, renowned for its delicacy and beauty, and which was centred upon the island of Unst. A factor in the development of the knitting traditions in the area has undoubtedly been the breed of sheep, said to have existed on the islands since the Stone Age. The dreadful weather and poor grazing land has produced a rugged animal with a surprisingly soft fleece which has good length fibres.

The wool was traditionally plucked from the animal by a technique referred to as rooing, rather than being shorn. When the cottagers process the wool for Shetland knitting, they tend to keep the yarn as natural as possibly by scouring but not dyeing it, the sheep themselves providing a range of most attractive natural colours, varying from light naturals to dark browns and through to black.

The Norwegian heritage has undoubtedly made its mark on the knitting in the Shetlands and Norwegian style symbols are to be found in the Shetland stitch patterns. Nevertheless, what are recognised as the traditional patterns today are perhaps only as old as the 1900s. There was a tendency for the patterns to cover the garment with the bands being kept to the same width throughout the garment and originally the colours used in these bands of pattern were more subtle than the bright colours used by Fair Isle knitters. The patterns are made more effective through the reversal of the colouring used on alternative bands of light and dark. Shetland patterns tend to be based on simple symmetrical and geometrical designs and tend to be based on diagonals rather than verticals, with a centre row knitted in one colour to provide an emphasis.

A peerie, or small pattern band, covers five or seven rows, and may be used in between wide bands or as part of a more complex pattern. The wider interim patterns are normally formed by between eleven and thirteen rows, including such symbols as crosses and stars as well as other motifs. The widest patterns cover twenty-five to thirty-one rows, and occasionally all-over patterns might be knitted.

Shetland Lace from the Island of Unst

To complete the story of Shetland knitting, lace knitting, made famous by the people of Unst, demands recognition.

From the seventeenth century, the island knitters, as well as knitting for family use, also produced fine stockings for export. Lace stockings were not

A Shetland lace shawl from the Island of Unst.

produced for their utility, but for fashion, and were sent hundreds of miles away to the sophisticated city centres of Edinburgh and London. Knitting of lace soon became an important source of income for some islanders, so much so that crofting had to be given up by the expert lace knitter who needed to have smooth hands for her work.

Exactly how lace knitting came to the islands is not recorded. In other chapters it has been seen that lace knitting had been practised in some parts of Europe, and it is possible that traders brought samples which influenced the development of this form of knitting on the island. It is suggested that when a certain Mrs Jessie Scanlon visited the islands early in the nineteenth century, she showed off her collection of fine lace from Brussels, Madeira and Valencia. The islanders were said to have been so inspired by its beauty that they extended their hand knitting skills to copy these patterns and developed the island's lace knitting as a result. Cowies *Guide to the Shetlands* published in 1870 mentions a parliamentary candidate there in the 1830s who sent a lace cap from the mainland to somebody on the islands as a present. It could have been this that was copied. This form of knitting must have been well established in Lerwick and Unst by the 1840s as stockings knitted in lace were being exported by this time. Patterns were passed on by word of mouth and given colourful and representative names, such as Bird's Eye, Cat's Paw, Horseshoe, Old Shale and Print of the Wave to represent features of life on

Passing a Shetland shawl through a wedding ring.

Three-cornered shoulder shawl from the Shetlands.

their island. It is said that often the lace knitter had no idea of which stitch she would use next, rather deciding by intuition as she finished the one she was making.

The fine long staple wool when plucked from the sheep produced a superb yarn ideal for the purpose of fine lace knitting. The merchant Edward Stanton commissioned a lace-knitted wedding veil produced from home-spun yarn from the island, which was shown at the Great Exhibition in 1851, but Shetland shawls had become prized possessions for evening wear in London society at least a decade before.

The lace knitter, taught by her mother whilst she was very young, would wear a leather knitting belt which had holes punched in it, to support the stationary needle as she worked. The expert knitter could reach a speed of up to two hundred stitches a minute. But the total labour needed to complete say, a shawl, might take five hundred hours. At an hourly rate of about threepence (1p) this was clearly not going to make fortunes. Using the traditional stitch patterns, such as those mentioned above, they might contain as many as one million stitches and measure some two metres square. In weight, however, a shawl might be as little as 85 grams (3 ozs). A shawl would be made using extremely fine needles, and after completion it would be soaked and hung on a special frame, either in the open or by a fire, to dry to the correct shape. A completed shawl could be so fine that it could be drawn through a wedding ring – hence the finest are known as ring shawls.

Fair Isle

Fair Isle lies in the stormy Pentland Firth between the Orkneys and the Scottish mainland. Its knitters have developed a distinctive tradition of their own. Although the islanders once had strong links with Scandinavia, Fair Isle has been part of Scotland for over five hundred years and in 1954 the island was acquired by the National Trust for Scotland. The island has long been famous for its brightly coloured knitwear which became fashionable in 1922, when the then Prince of Wales was seen playing golf at St Andrews wearing a racy Fair Isle pullover under a jacket. Then, as today, Royalty set the trend in fashionable wear and when the Prince added to the interest in Fair Isle knitting, spinners in the inter-war period included many designs featuring Fair Isle-type stitch patterns in their range of knitting leaflets.

Some claim that the distinctive stitches of the island developed from the time when the flagship of the Spanish Armada, *El Gran Grifon,* was wrecked in a storm off its shores in 1588 and it has been suggested that the islanders imitated Spanish insignia in their knitting. There are, however, similarities between Nordic and Fair Isle knitting styles, due possibly to the past associations of these two peoples. Fair Isle stitch patterns have romantic names such as the Armada Cross and the Rose of Sharon. As in the Shetland Islands, local wool was used in traditional Fair Isle knitting, being carded, spun and dyed by the cottagers.

A romantic story from James Norbury concerns the practice of a Fair Isle grandmother producing the first traditionally patterned pullover for her adolescent grandsons to wear, called a Robe of Glory. It would start with a plain rib and then continue in patterning all the way up. The first band would probably be some variant on the Water of Life, immediately followed by the Seed of Life and the Flower of Life, these indicating the happy growth of the wearer to maturity. Aspirations for the wearer might then be represented by a band showing the Anchor of Hope, and then there would be a band of a Star pattern to guide the wearer on his way through life. The culmination towards, or at, the shoulders would be the Crown of Glory band as the ultimate reward to be gained through living a good and virtuous life.

Fair Isle knitting probably started as recently as the middle of the nineteenth century, when the dyeing of bright colours was made possible through imported dyes and new techniques in fixing. This was also the time when stranding of colour knitting was mastered in the area. Islanders with a knowledge of that period said that a Fair Isle sailor returned home with a brightly patterned shawl from one of the Baltic ports, the stitch colouring of which was copied, adopted and adapted by the local knitters.

The Channel Isles
In Chapter 11 there was a discussion of guernsey or gansey knitting. Although named after the second largest Channel Isle, it may or may not have originated there – the name may merely have been used to designate a garment similar to that worn by the island's fishermen. The craft of knitting was well developed in France and the knitters in ports quite close to the Channel Islands, such as those in Brittany, had developed some form of gansey knitting, which may have influenced the island knitters.

From the two larger islands in the group have come names which are now immortalised in the language of knitwear – Jersey and Guernsey. Both are pullover types of garment, and both started life being worn by the fishermen of the two islands. The word jersey has now come to mean an article of knitwear, and is somewhat general in application, whereas the guernsey, has remained a rather special jumper, belonging to the fishermen.

Knitting in these islands is a long established tradition, and records tell of exports of hand-knitted articles from Jersey since the days when Sir Walter Raleigh was Governor there. It is suggested that in 1557 Queen Mary (Tudor) graciously accepted a gift of a number of knitted items from an earlier Governor and her sister and successor Queen Elizabeth I also had a pair of Guernsey hose in her wardrobe. The ill-fated Mary Stuart, Queen of Scots, it is said, wore a pair of white Guernsey hose when she mounted the block for her execution. In the eighteenth century, up to a quarter of a million pairs of hose made by the Guernsey knitters were being exported annually.

The Guernsey has some features which distinguish it from other ganseys. First the welt has a slit on either side, to give more freedom of movement, and secondly, it is generally knitted plain, the knitter producing perfectly even stocking stitch in the process.

The Island Knitters and Fashion
Today, the traditional patterns from the islands of Aran, Shetland and Fair Isle, as well as the Channel Islands, have become trendsetters in fashion. Hand knits based firmly on traditional island designs have made regular appearances and as such have helped to keep the tradition of island knitting alive.

CHAPTER 13
Patons and Fashion in Handknitting

Earlier chapters have included contributions on the development of handknitting design over the past hundred years or so. Dealing with these examples piecemeal does not really show the dramatic changes that have occurred in knitting fashions from the last decade of the nineteenth century until today. In this period, especially more recently with the advent of the mass media and personality cults, famous people have frequently had an influence on the public's response to design. Her Majesty Queen Elizabeth has been photographed wearing a handknitted Aran cardigan. Prince Charles, The Prince of Wales, appeared in a beautifully knitted Fair Isle pullover on the BBC TV programme Jackanory in 1984. This was knitted in red, white and blue and as well as anchor and star patterns, included a row of crowns and the knitted initials C and D, for Charles and his wife Diana. Princess Diana added to the interest in motif knitting when she wore the now famous sweater featuring numerous white sheep motifs with one black one amongst them.

The designs in knitting leaflets tend to fall into two categories – garments produced with functional purposes in mind, and those which emphasise fashion. In an earlier chapter the publication of early knitting instructions was discussed; by the middle nineteenth century small books of knitting designs were quite common. Women's magazines had become well established by the beginning of this century and because most are published on a weekly or monthly basis, they can respond quickly to changes in fashion, and so produce an up-to-the-minute reflection of the fashion scene. Spinners, for their part, had started to contribute their booklets or pamphlets of instructions in the 1890s.

The great leap forward in the popularising of the women's press was the Education Act of 1870, which promoted literacy on a hitherto unknown scale. At the same time printing techniques were improving. And the two distinct, yet related, factors encouraged reading amongst the working classes for the first time. In addition, paper was becoming relatively cheap and the development of an efficient national network of distribution meant that publications could actually reach the general public in the great industrial centres that had developed during the Industrial Revolution.

Woman's Weekly first appeared in 1911 and after initial success met with a period of stagnation. Then Biddy Johnson was asked to step in as editor and remodel the journal. She told the publisher that provided she was given a free hand, with a basic content of knitting and fiction, she could make the magazine successful once more. This she did, and by 1930 the circulation was over half a million, rising to one million copies soon after.

At about the same time *Woman* and *Woman's Own* were first published and were innovative in that they aimed at the younger woman who, following the social changes brought about by the First World War, now had growing financial independence. Magazine content changed from a concentration on home crafts and fiction to interest in fashion and style and, in accommodating the expectations of this new element of women's magazine readership, magazine circulation as a whole was further increased.

The high-fashion magazines appeared at about the same time – *Vogue* was first published in Great Britain in 1916, and was, indeed still is, in the forefront of fashion. As well as the general mass circulation weeklies, specialist monthlies such as *Pins and Needles* and Patons' *Stitchcraft*, which was first published in October 1932, covered all needlecrafts but with an emphasis on knitting designs.

Improvements in dyeing techniques ensured both fastness and an increase in the range of colours available, which enabled the impact of colour on fashion to become more important. As in any period, certain shades attracted special interest or favour at different times.

Taking examples from the many thousands of different designs produced by Patons & Baldwins, both as separate entities and after their merger, this chapter will trace trends in the design of handknits. In this it is noticeable that a number of classics have withstood the test of time and other, novelty designs have enjoyed instant success – and sunk, never to reappear!

The Eighteen-Nineties

The Naughty Nineties

The tail end of the Victorian era saw a distillation in fashion of much that had gone before. The hourglass figure, with its tiny corsetted waist and exaggerated bust and hipline, was seen in its most extreme form at this time. Leg-of-mutton sleeves had replaced simple fitted sleeves by the middle of the decade. There was also an emphasis on pleating and frills. In all this the visual effect was of paramount importance, with little regard to comfort or health.

But changes were on the way. In the past, sport had generally been considered unsuitable for women, but as the twentieth century approached attitudes were changing. Women were taking up cycling, golf, tennis and other outdoor activities requiring more flexibility of movement than the usual day wear could afford and so knitting came into its own. In her book on costumes, Doreen Yarwood writes that 'Woolies in the form of knitted cardigans and waistcoats began to make their appearance in the nineties, especially for sportswear'.

For much of the Victorian period the colours used had tended to be fairly vivid, although Queen Victoria herself wore black. However, the 1890s saw a move away from the vibrant blues, magentas and greens and a steady trend towards the darker, muted shades. Brown, navy blue and black were much favoured at this time. Knitting designs of the period reflected this rather sombre atmosphere in practical, hard wearing designs – in colours that would not show the dirt! Patons and Baldwins were operating separately in this period and in 1896 Patons published a booklet of knitting instructions entitled *The Knitting and Crochet Book*. In this there were instructions for many underclothes and smaller items, such as socks and gloves, but the designs for jumpers, cardigans and capes tended to follow simple lines.

The Nineteen-Sixties

PATONS 101 Courtelle Double Crepe 9700 9d
One size to fit 34-36 inch bust
Mary Quant Courtelle

PATONS 101 Courtelle Double Crepe 9701 9d
One size to fit 34-36 inch bust
Mary Quant Courtelle

C-1094 6d
Chelsea Sweaters in Double Knittings by P & B in six sizes for man or woman 34-44 in.

9006 9d
Patons Big Ben Knitting
Three sizes to fit 26-30 inch chest

The Nineteen-Seventies

The Nineteen-Eighties

The Eighteen-Nineties

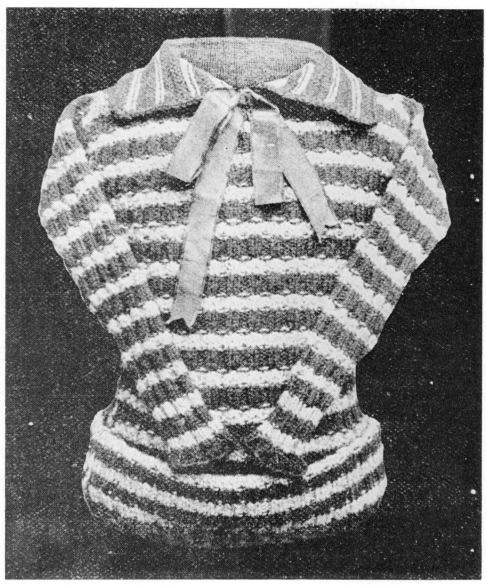

Boys jersey with turn-over collar 1896.

The Princess of Wales in her now-famous 'Black Sheep' sweater

The Eighteen-Nineties

Sweater, 1896.

The Nineteen-Hundreds

Edwardian Elegance

The two firms continued to operate independently, each having now been in business for about one hundred years. They had separately recognised the benefit of the knitting yarn spinner. producing clear instructions for the knitter. This decade saw the beginning of the building up of a list of booklets and leaflets of instructions for knitters who used their yarns.

This was also the period when the ideas associated with women's emancipation developed apace. These were the days of the valiant Suffragettes, when Edith New chained herself to the railings of 10 Downing Street to gain public attention, and when the movement was given determined leadership by Mrs Emmeline Pankhurst and her daughters.

Until the end of the Victorian age the design of women's clothes had placed an emphasis on the accentuated feminine figure, but social and economic trends are often echoed in fashion and, as women became more aware of their potential contribution to society in different roles, so came the realisation that crinolines, bustles and corsets presented a most impractical, uncomfortable obstacle to their aspirations. Knitting designs, however, continued to be practical and essentially simple rather than closely following fashion trends.

The yarns used by knitters in this period tended to be three- and four-ply in the main although two-ply was also in demand for those special finer items. The exception was Patons Wheeling, which was woollen spun and about a double knitting thickness. The lines of garments tended to copy classical looks and in spite of the gaiety of the Edwardian age, the knitter still concentrated on the production of basic goods rather than elaborate, fashion items. Colouring tended to be subdued rather than bright.

The Nineteen-Hundreds

BEEHIVE KNITTING BOOKLETS No. 10.

LADY'S CAP & RAGLAN JACKET

Knitted in an easy fancy Stitch from

TRADE MARK **BB**

BEEHIVE DOUBLE KNITTING WOOL

J. & J. BALDWIN & PARTNERS LTD.
HALIFAX
ENGLAND
ESTABLISHED 1785

PRICE ONE PENNY (or by post 1½d.)

The Nineteen-Hundreds

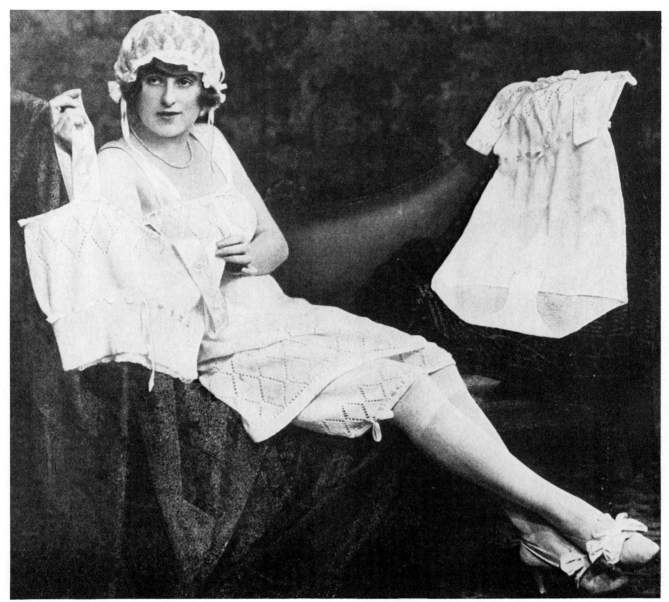

Lady's knitted underwear.

The Nineteen-Tens

Women's Rights and Austerity
This period takes the two firms of Patons and Baldwins up to the time when they merged. By now the drive for women's enfranchisement was gaining popular sympathy and in 1918 a limited number of women over thirty were given the vote. Women over twenty-one did not get the vote until 1928.

The Great War finally bade farewell to the Victorian age of glory and opened a period of changing values and expectations of society. The huge numerical imbalance of the sexes caused by the loss of millions of young men led to many more career possibilities for single women, many of whom also sought new fashions of dress. In fashion, however, the hem line continued to hover just above the ground, in spite of wartime shortages. It should be remembered that women had worn ankle or floor length garments for centuries and it was to take radical changes in attitude to alter this. The country's austerity measures were reflected instead in the quality and choice of material — colours were drab, and designs practical.

Before the middle of this period the first edition of *Woolcraft* was issued by Baldwins. *Woolcraft*, like the *Universal Knitting Book*, was packed with hints to help the knitter. Knitting designs did not alter greatly through the period, since fashion was not so volatile as today and the fashion lines of the day were in regular use for the first twenty years of the century.

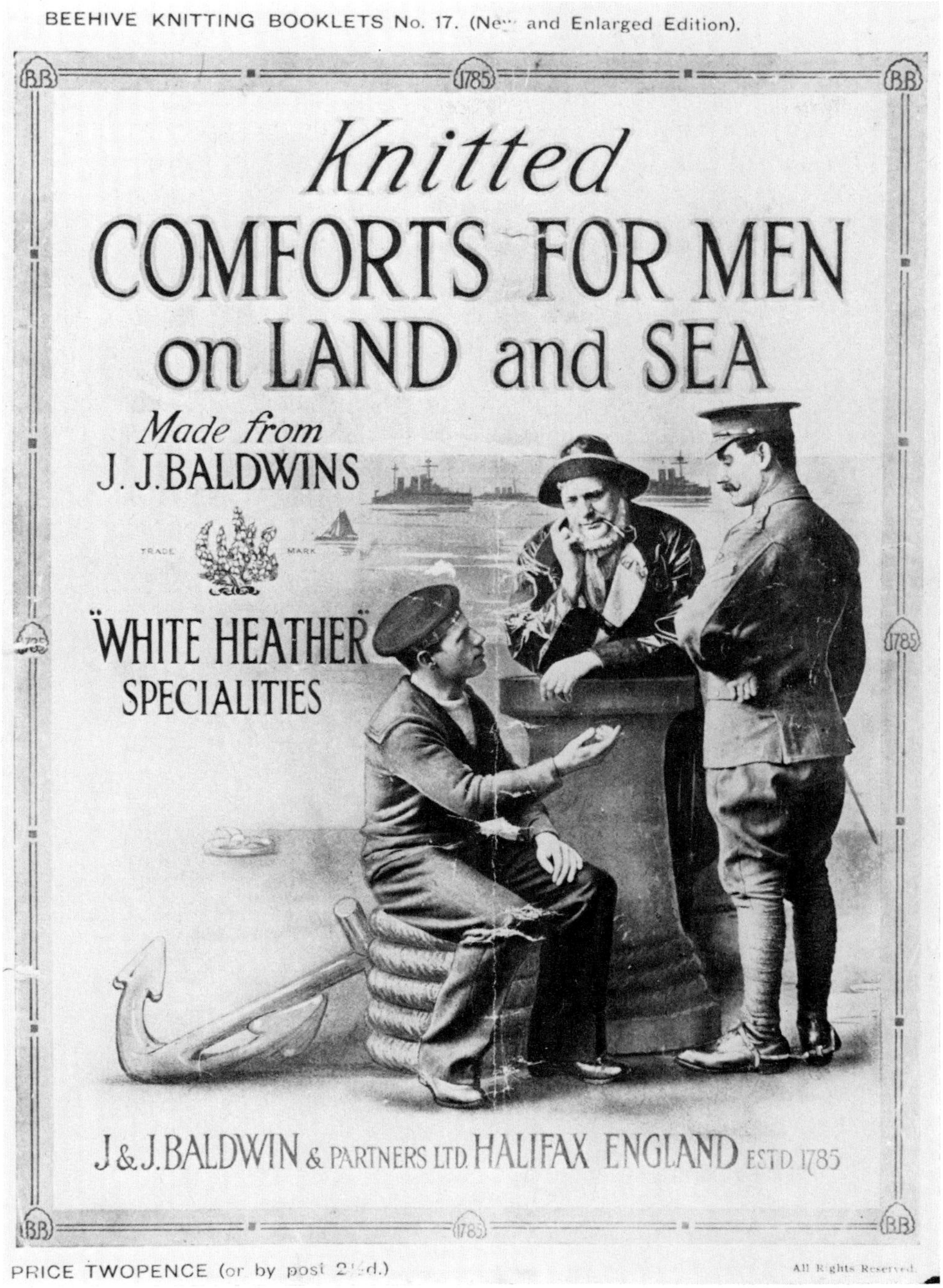

Knitted comforts for the troops, 1914.

The Nineteen-Tens

The Nineteen-Twenties

Youth, Chastity and the Flapper
In 1920 the two firms had merged to become Patons & Baldwins Limited. The end of the Great War, with the major social and economic upheavals it brought about, also unleashed a spirit of pent-up gaiety amongst the youth of the country, a feeling of living for the moment. In retrospect this was to be short-lived, as despair and despondency returned all too quickly with the Depression.

The silhouette in the early Twenties was dramatically different from previous styles. Dresses were narrow tubes, devoid of shaping and designed to disguise the natural contours of the body. The bust was flattened to give a boyish look, the waist was lost altogether and only a sash or belt gave an indication of the hipline. Hairstyles also followed the androgynous theme with women cutting their hair short and adopting quasi-masculine looks. Cosmetics, which in the previous hundred and thirty years had only been used by prostitutes and theatrical people, now gained general acceptance and were used widely. The overall impression was one of health and vitality, and short sleeves and shorter hemlines demanded cover-ups in the form of cardigans or jumpers which adopted the same long lean lines. Colours tended to be muted and pastel.

Handknits could be used to 'camouflage' a woman's natural shape. Jumpers and cardigans were designed to make the natural lines of bust, waist and hips into one. The result was to remove definition from the individual's form, while allowing complete comfort. The use of stocking stitch for garments emphasised the simplicity of line used, although motif interest was occasionally introduced by the use of monograms or initials. This period saw the dawn of the fashionable sleeveless pullover for men, particularly in Fair Isle styles made popular by Edward, the then Prince of Wales.

The Nineteen-Twenties

The Nineteen-Twenties

The Nineteen-Thirties

Figures and Femininity

This was the decade when the world experienced and came out of a Depression — and was on the brink of another World War. It was also a decade when everybody seemed to knit. The Twenties' boyish look gave way to a voluptuously feminine look, in which the bust was exaggerated. Femininity in its most glamorous sense returned, with figure-hugging garments coming into vogue — and knitting lent itself perfectly to the production of these. In those years the waistline made a reappearance with garments shaped at the side seams and worn with wide belts to create the clinched look. The Mid-Thirties saw padded shoulders make an entrance and these served to emphasise even further the narrowness of a woman's waist.

Hairstyles could never return to the elaborate confections of an earlier time of leisure, and so remained fairly short. Curls were worn in abundance. Cosmetics had been refined by now and their use was more subtle, with the emphasis moving from eyes to lips.

Doreen Yarwood wrote that 'jumpers and cardigans ... increased in popularity towards 1939, when a jumper, often home-knitted, and a skirt became the favourite attire for many women'. Twinsets, which have recently enjoyed something of a revival, were also a staple of any woman's wardrobe. Puffed sleeves became popular, as did frivolous trimmings and stitch patterns to add interest to garments. Geometric designs, which have been noted as a popular tradition in many countries, came into favour with the fashionable in the 1930s. The use of colour was initially adopted by men but was gradually taken over by women as well, especially for sweaters to be worn for sporting activities such as golf or hiking.

Knitting was being used to produce fashionable garments, so when in 1932 Patons & Baldwins Limited introduced the magazine *Stitchcraft*, with a fashion emphasis, it became an instant success.

The Nineteen-Thirties

The Nineteen-Thirties

The Nineteen-Forties

The Watershed and the New Look
The world was at war again. The outcome was to increase the production of off-the-peg clothes and for the garments themselves to be more practical still. Knitting yarns were difficult to obtain, so frequently old garments had to be unravelled and knitted anew. Times were very hard indeed, and fashion reflected this mood of severity. Utility was the order of the day and rationing continued until well after the conflict was over.

Men's clothing in the preceding seventy years or so had tended to be generally conservative and sombre, with the notable exception of the royal influence on Fair Isle slipovers in the twenties. At the end of the Second World War, when uniforms could be discarded, there was a move away from the dull and dreary styles and colours. Jackets and cardigans became looser, colour became more adventurous, sports jackets were more acceptable for day wear and woollen cardigans and pullovers were popular. The move towards more casual clothes for men was well on the way.

In 1947 the revolutionary 'New Look' from Christian Dior dictated longer skirts – twenty seven to thirty centimetres above the ground, and a pronounced bustline and tiny waist. Batwing sleeves also made an impact, and although styles had to be practicable as there were still shortages, the accent was on feminity. Hair remained short but was swept up and back in an illusion of a longer style. The New Look really took off in the late 1940s. It captured popular imagination and was a great morale booster in trying times.

Although nylon had been invented in 1928, its commercial push in the UK only came after import restrictions were imposed on Japanese silk immediately prior to the Second World War. Wartime research had many spin-offs, one being the improvement of nylon yarns, and a range of synthetic fibres followed.

Knitting designs during the war followed clear, uncluttered lines – it had to, for economy was of paramount importance. On the unveiling of the New Look, surface interest came to the fore, with the use of bobbles and moss-stitch being examples of the day's trend.

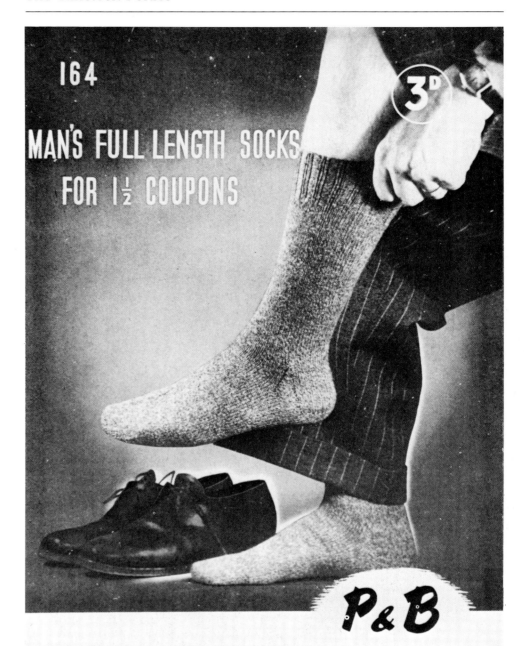

The Nineteen-Forties

163 PATONS BEEHIVE FINGERING, 2-PLY 3ᴰ
("Patonised" shrink-resist finish)

The Nineteen-Fifties

Simple, Short and Straight
This decade really started off under the heavy influence of Dior's New Look. Continental fashions became important and the French designers enjoyed a period of great eminence.

From the 1950s, handknitting fashion blossomed as double knitting became established as the basic thickness for yarns with some use of even heavier yarns. Double knittings also helped to establish knitting as a widespread pastime, as it was quicker to knit than the previously more popular 3 and 4 plys. Instructions had also become more easy to follow, the pre-war leaflets having tended to assume some expertise on the part of the knitter. Chunkies first became popular in the late 1950s, although the fashion for these had to wait until the early 1960s to reach its peak. Fashion became much less exclusive. It was in this period, in 1956, that Patons' "million seller" leaflet SC44 was first published, having sold well over three million copies since then and still going strong some thirty years later.

This was the period when Patons & Baldwins' Chief Designer, James Norbury, came to the fore. He had a regular column in a national newspaper of the day, the Daily Herald, and through his appearances on BBC TV soon became known as "TV's Knitting Man". He and his designs had a tremendous influence on the fashions for handknits.

The Nineteen-Fifties

In 1956 this leaflet first appeared. It is still going strong thirty years later, with sales of over three million copies.

The Nineteen-Sixties

The Swinging Sixties
Continental influence remained strong during this period, but the emphasis had shifted from France to include Italy and Spain. Fashion lines continued to get simpler and less fussy. There were two main trends – one was to obscure the waistline completely in, say, a shift-like dress, or alternatively to emphasise it with swirling skirts tightly belted. Britain had enjoyed a period of peace and relative prosperity. Certainly a feeling of confidence and optimism carried over into the wild and carefree fashions of the Sixties. Colours were bright and gay – eventually to become psychedelic! Hair was either worn extremely long, or very short.

The undisputed trademark of the Sixties was the mini-skirt. What may have been considered outrageous only a decade before became a sign of the new woman's confidence, her desire to dress in a style which defied convention and outraged parents. It was nothing short of a social revolution – youngsters could no longer be expected to respect tradition.

Handknits became a fashion in their own right, with the emphasis on the use of chunky yarns, with Patons Big Ben leading the way to make garments particularly for outdoor wear. Fancy yarns which gave great surface interest also started to show up in significant numbers.

The Nineteen-Seventies

Knitting as a Fashion in Casual Wear
Although the 'Swinging Sixties' passed as a brief kaleidoscopic interlude, they left their mark on the Seventies; the heritage passed down was of greater independence of spirit.

Teenagers of the Sixties became mothers in the Seventies, and just as other expectations were raised, so were their demands from knitting designs and yarns. Colour, stitch pattern and texture were all important. Texture was emphasised with the growth of brushed yarns which provided the biggest single change in knitting in the decade. The mini was followed by the midi in the 1970s – a hemline of approximately calf-length. This was followed briefly by the maxi, or full length garment. There will always be adherents to the current fad or gimmick, but the modern woman can afford to choose what she feels will suit her best and is not restricted to the mood of the moment.

The brevity of the mini skirt had a swansong in the hot pant craze of the early Seventies, frequently worn with knitted bolero-type tops. A major trend was the adoption of jeans. This continues today and has led to a significant relaxation of attitudes towards 'acceptable wear'. For long it was unthinkable for a woman to wear trousers.

Spinners moved into a competitive market. Chunkies had lost some popularity by the beginning of this decade, the exception being Aran yarns, with Patons' Capstan leading the way. Double knitting became the standard, and colour and texture combined to highlight fashionable design. Emphasis was on the production of colour-conscious fashion yarns, which blended different fibres.

The Nineteen-Eighties

Patons, Leader in Fashion
It is much easier to look back on a period for its most outstanding characteristics than to try and highlight what are contemporary movements. Hot pants have turned into knickerbockers, culottes, bermudas. The Eighties have seen Punks, Ethnics and New Romantics, three distinct trends, but there is also a predominance of casual wear. Dressing in whatever is comfortable has found favour.

Patons have experimented with different fibres for yarns — both natural and exciting blends. Cotton has been in vogue in the early part of the decade, particularly for summer wear. Pastels have been favourites, showing again the emphasis on colour and texture rather than on the line of the design, and the interest in brushed yarns continues.

POSTSCRIPT
What Will The Future Bring?

This book has traced the story of handknitting from its origins and its spread throughout the world. The craft's history spans some two thousand years; its development and its emergence as an industry have been described, as has its culmination as an art form in certain periods and areas. Since the decline of handknitting as an industry it has become firmly established as a leisure pursuit. A question that can only be answered as time unfolds is what the future holds in store for knitting.

At the moment all the ingredients are there for it to continue as a leisure pursuit. The spinners of knitting yarns, particularly, have developed the ability to identify fashions and trends in knitters' preferences and to react quickly. The media are also likely to keep this interest buoyant. Television has, as yet, hardly touched on possible ways of exploiting the visual aspects of knitting, in fashion, for instance, or as a teaching medium, although there have been programmes on the craft for many years. The new form of presenting the text of knitting instructions through the TV screens in Teletext has yet to be exploited.

Women's magazines continue to highlight the craft; Biddy Johnson's statement about the importance of woman's fiction and knitting in maintaining their circulation is as valid today as it was when it was made in 1911.

On the distribution front the specialist woolshop has become well established and there are many other outlets for knitters' products, the departmental stores, mail order and the non-specialist retailer who carries knitting yarns. However, changes in the face of retailing since the Second World War have been as spectacular as changes in technology, so it is difficult to guess what face retailing will show in ten years time, let alone a century or more.

The Knitting Environment
It is the interest of members of the human race in knitting that really provides the key. Why do people knit?

First consider the environment in which the knitter lives, the main components of which are natural, social and economic, and the pyschological reasons for knitting. In countries such as Great Britain, and more so in North America, there is a variable climate. The winters are moderately cold, and the summers, although warmer, have temperatures which drop considerably at night. There is a need for warm clothing, but climatic factors may diminish in importance.

Moving on to the social aspect, knitting equipment can be carried in a small bag and knitting can take place anywhere with little inconvenience – knitting is mobile. It is socially acceptable to do it almost anywhere in non-formal, and even in some formal, gatherings. People can chat and knit, listen and knit, and travel and knit. Women's organisations give an impetus to knitting. People will knit for charity; blankets for the deprived in developing countries; sponsored 'knit-ins' – the satisfaction in all this is great and at the same time others are being helped.

Knitting is a craft that can be easily learned. Daughters see mothers knitting and want to copy them. Children will be taught to knit at school. Everybody who wants to knit can learn.

Society breeds fashion, so fashion becomes another aspect of knitting. As well as environment, culture and mood affect what is knitted. If there is a trend towards discovering roots, the ethnic look will come in; if it's 'back to nature', the home-spun look is favoured; or high fashion may be the vogue. It can all be interpreted by knitting – and tailored and coloured to the knitter's taste and size as a unique self-made article.

There are the economic aspects of knitting. One only requires a pair of inexpensive needles, and the yarn to be knitted. The cost of the knitter's labour is more or less free. Handknitted goods tend to be cheaper than machine-made equivalents for similar quality. As agriculture and industry become more productive through the application of new technology, fewer hours will be worked. Then hobbies such as knitting can be used even more to fill the increasing leisure time.

Concerning psychological factors, knitting is said to have a therapeutic effect. It is soothing and can help one relax, assuming the knitter does not select too complicated a set of instructions to follow. Above all, there is the need many have to create, and knitting is creative. Choice of design, colour selection, knitting the fabric and the final product are the creation of the knitter, which leads to a great satisfaction being obtained from the completed garment.

All the signs point to the availability of the skills, the time and the materials necessary to enable the craft to be carried out. Perhaps the environment is firmly established to take knitters over the next 200 years.